SECURITY ARCHITECT

BCS, THE CHARTERED INSTITUTE FOR IT

BCS, The Chartered Institute for IT, champions the global IT profession and the interests of individuals engaged in that profession for the benefit of all. We promote wider social and economic progress through the advancement of information technology science and practice. We bring together industry, academics, practitioners and government to share knowledge, promote new thinking, inform the design of new curricula, shape public policy and inform the public.

Our vision is to be a world-class organisation for IT. Our 70,000 strong membership includes practitioners, businesses, academics and students in the UK and internationally. We deliver a range of professional development tools for practitioners and employees. A leading IT qualification body, we offer a range of widely recognised qualifications.

Further Information
BCS The Chartered Institute for IT,
First Floor, Block D,
North Star House, North Star Avenue,
Swindon, SN2 1FA, United Kingdom.
T +44 (0) 1793 417 424
F +44 (0) 1793 417 444
www.bcs.org/contact

http://shop.bcs.org/

SECURITY ARCHITECT
Careers in IT service management

Jon Collins

Published by BCS Learning & Development Ltd, a wholly owned subsidiary of BCS, The Chartered Institute for IT, First Floor, Block D, North Star House, North Star Avenue, Swindon, SN2 1FA, UK.
www.bcs.org

Paperback ISBN: 978-1-78017-220-0
PDF ISBN: 978-1-78017-221-7
ePUB ISBN: 978-1-78017-222-4
Kindle ISBN: 978-1-78017-223-1

Ebook
available

British Cataloguing in Publication Data.
A CIP catalogue record for this book is available at the British Library.

BCS books are available at special quantity discounts to use as premiums and sale promotions, or for use in corporate training programs. Please visit our Contact Us page at www.bcs.org/contact

Typeset by Lapiz Digital Services, Chennai, India.

In memory of Neil Wybrow.

CONTENTS

LIST OF FIGURES

AUTHOR'S NOTE

The information security world was rocked in 2012 when a number of revelations came to light about the full extent of government surveillance in the US, UK and elsewhere. As a result a number of concerns have arisen among security professionals, not least the potential for 'back doors' in some commonly used encryption algorithms, which could be exploited by government entities. Despite these revelations, the basic premise behind information security in general, and the role of encryption in particular, remain as important as ever.

ACKNOWLEDGEMENTS

The author would like to express his thanks to Matthew Flynn and Jutta Mackwell at BCS, and Dan Webster at National Trust for his feedback and contributions. Also Steve Greenham, Adrian Seccombe and all those at the illustrious Jericho Forum, Gareth Fraser-King and Guy Bunker, as well as Nick Gleich, Nigel Wilmott, Pio Reindl, John Piper, Gary Shrubb and all those at AMSL, Peter Fischer and Mike Stubbings at GCHQ/CESG for past guidance.

ABBREVIATIONS

AES	Advanced Encryption Standard
ANSI	American National Standards Institute
BC	Business Continuity
BCP	Business Continuity Plan
BS	British Standard
BYOD	Bring Your Own Device
CESG	Communications-Electronics Security Group
CLEF	Commercial Licensed Evaluation Facility
CMS	Content Management System
COBIT	Control OBjectives for Information and related Technology
CPD	Continuous Professional Development
CRM	Customer Relationship Management
CSA	Cloud Security Alliance
CSIA	Central Sponsor for Information Assurance
DDoS	Distributed Denial of Service
DES	Data Encryption Standard
DMZ	De-Militarised Zone
DoD	US Department of Defense
DoS	Denial of Service
DPA	Data Protection Act
DR	Disaster Recovery
EU	European Union
GCHQ	Government Communications Headquarters

HR	Human Resources
IA	Information Assurance
ICT	Information and Communications Technologies
IDEF	Integrated Computer-Aided Manufacturing (ICAM) DEFinition
IDS	Intrusion Detection System
ISO	International Organization for Standardization
ISMS	Information Security Management System
ITIL	Information Technology Infrastructure Library
ITSEC	Information Technology Security Evaluation Criteria
ITU	International Telecommunications Union
LAN	Local Area Network
PCI-DSS	Payment Card Industry – Data Security Standard
PIN	Personal Identification Number
SANS	SysAdmin, Audit, Network, Security Institute
SCADA	Supervisory Control And Data Acquisition
SFIA	Skills Framework for the Information Age
SLA	Service Level Agreement
SSL	Secure Sockets Layer
VM	Virtual Machine
VPN	Virtual Private Network
WAN	Wide Area Network
Wi-Fi	Wireless Fidelity

GLOSSARY

Short definitions of key terms and concepts follow. These include General Information Assurance Products and Services Initiative definitions, which in turn have been taken, in order, from BS ISO/ IEC 27001:2005, ISO/IEC FDIS 13335-1 or ISO/IEC 27002:2013, other ISO standards, or from SC27 and SD6 standards.

Anonymisation The (usually automated) process of replacing private information with similar information which cannot be used to identify the person involved or their details. For example, a name and address could be replaced with a generic name and an address in a similar neighbourhood.

Asset A physical object, software or data item which is of tangible value to the organisation.

Audit trail A corpus of information and records including log data, signed forms and supporting materials that can provide evidence as to whether a security procedure was followed appropriately in relation to a specific event.

Authentication The process of demonstrating that a user or system has valid credentials, usually to enable access to a computer system, application or service.

Authorisation The process of giving access to a system, service, application or information source based on the presentation of a valid identity.

Availability The ability to access a computer system, service, application or information item. In security circles the term usually refers to information availability, but the term is broadened in systems management to refer to system resilience.

Certificate authority   A third-party body which can verify the authenticity of both a **public key certificate** and its source.

Confidentiality   The assurance that information is kept in a state where unauthorised people or systems cannot view or access it.

De-militarised zone (DMZ)   This is a part of the network which is neither on the public network, nor the more secure enterprise network. It is used to locate enterprise controlled elements of IT which operate under different security conditions to corporate systems, for example websites.

Data loss/leakage prevention or protection   A software-based mechanism, potentially delivered as an appliance, which enables data and messages (such as web-based data and emails) to be scanned as they leave the trusted corporate zone, to prevent sensitive data from exiting.

Defence in depth   The use of multiple security controls and mechanisms in a layered approach to augment the overall security of the ICT environment.

Encryption   A process to encode data items (at rest or in transit) so that they are meaningless to any person or system that lacks the decryption key.

Enterprise architecture   The activities, models and approaches relating to the design and representation of complex organisations and the technologies used to support them.

Firewall   A software-based mechanism used to detect, filter and report network communications that are unauthorised, unwanted and/or not from a trusted source.

Hacker A person who deliberately attempts to breach the security of an organisation. Hackers may be distinguished as 'black hat', acting maliciously, or 'white hat', acting for the good of, and potentially being paid by, the organisation concerned.

Identity management The approach and process linked to assigning unique characteristics to individuals or objects which can then be used as part of **authentication** and/or **authorisation**.

Integrity The assurance that information has not been modified, corrupted or otherwise changed from its original or expected state.

Least privilege A system design principle which works on the basis of only giving access to the information and/or resources deemed necessary for a particular task, purpose or role.

Public key certificate An electronic document that enables a web server to accept HTTPS connections, or to verify that a public key belongs to an individual.

Secure Hypertext Transfer Protocol (HTTPS) An http connection encrypted using Secure Sockets Layer or Transport Layer Security algorithms.

Security zone A well-bounded area of the physical or logical IT environment, which serves as a basis for protective measures and security controls.

Separation of duties A principle which requires more than one person to be involved in a task, in order to minimise the risk of fraud, misdemeanour or human error.

Social engineering An element of security breaches involving playing on human weakness, for example by suggesting clicking on an apparently innocuous link in an email.

Trust level   A grouping of criteria applied to people or system services, to enable policies to be set for a given system or application, physical space or **security zone**. To achieve a trust level may require accreditation or vetting of a system or person respectively.

Virtual private network (VPN)   An encrypted networking connection, which exists as a secure 'tunnel', enabling **confidential** traffic to run across an insecure network outside of a trusted **security zone**.

White hat hacker   See hacker.

PREFACE

WHY DO WE NEED INFORMATION SECURITY ARCHITECTURE?

A few years ago, a number of pundits (such as Carr 2003) suggested that information technology (IT) was being commoditised and, therefore, no longer needed to be treated as strategic. In the same vein, one could be forgiven for thinking that information security principles and standards have already been worked out.

Recent developments such as cloud computing, virtualisation, big data, social networking, mobile and home working, as well as the globalisation of markets and other demographic changes, have illustrated that nothing could be further from the truth. Such huge shifts in both technology and behaviour have completely changed the way we think about information technology in general, and information security in particular.

The most significant consequence is that the days of thinking about security on a piecemeal basis, in terms of threat-preventing products, are well and truly over. Across the past decade we have seen the field of information security architecture emerge, based on efforts by security professionals to build a more comprehensive, strategic view of security which considers the IT environment as a whole, rather than treating it on a system-by-system basis.

While the basic principles behind security architecture might not be new (we have long used analogies of chains being only as strong as the weakest link, for example) the security architect role is relatively recent and the discipline lacks generally accepted standards. As a result, organisations have divergent views on what security architecture represents, and the activities involved in its deployment.

The purpose of this book, therefore, is to provide a foundation level of knowledge about security architecture, its purpose and approach. It presents the competences, skills and techniques required by security architects – as we shall see, these go way beyond the technical. The security architect's role is one of helping ensure that, in a complex and rapidly changing environment, both existing and new threats can be mitigated.

Above all, the security architect needs to be pragmatic, an expert in the art of the possible. Information security exists primarily to enable the business to function effectively: too much security and the overheads become onerous and are more likely to be ignored; too little and the core assets of the organisation remain exposed.

In this day and age, organisations cannot afford to leave information security to chance, and 'security by obscurity' – the InfoSec equivalent of assuming that bad things only ever happen to other people – is no longer an option. IT has never been as dynamic as today, and an architectural view of information security has become essential to minimising information and business risks across the IT environment, and hence the organisation as a whole.

1 INTRODUCTION

The ways businesses and people use technology today have created a state of paradox. Companies are trying to protect their core information assets and intellectual property while using externally hosted services, collaborating with partners and adopting agile, 'fail fast' approaches to business;[1] employees are using their own devices and exchanging corporate data via social tools; consumers are looking for more privacy at the same time as sometimes being accused of over-sharing.

As a result it has become difficult, if not impossible, to identify the boundaries of what was once termed 'corporate IT'. Today's technology environments need to encompass in-house data centres and cloud service providers, home desktops and facilities in airport lounges, smartphones and tablet computers, mobile networks and the wider internet.

In addition, technology is changing rapidly, creating a constant stream of headaches for anyone trying to secure it. While it is possible to identify today's generation of solutions, it is quite a stretch to imagine what will be in place in even two years' time as wave upon wave of innovations crash on the corporate landscape. A few years ago cloud computing was filling the column inches; then came big data and smart analytics; and today, the Internet of Things is the latest 'new thing'. Each augments, rather than replaces, the generations of technology that have gone before it.

---

[1] http://www.forbes.com/sites/nyuentrepreneurschallenge/2012/10/16/fail-fast-succeed-faster/

Against this background, how can organisations consider information security? The genie is quite clearly out of the bottle: it no longer makes sense to simply 'secure' an application, device or data set and see the job as done. Rather, each element needs to be considered as part of a broader technological ecosystem.

Enter the information security architect, whose job is to make sense of it all and offer the best possible advice to organisations looking to minimise technology-related risks.

THE ESSENCE OF SECURITY ARCHITECTURE

At its heart, information security brings together three well-established concepts – to preserve the confidentiality, integrity and availability of an organisation's information assets. However, in this day and age, we need all standards, policies, mechanisms and approaches relating to IT – information security included – to function across our globally distributed, highly fragmented technology environments. As a result good security practices are becoming increasingly architectural, in that an understanding of the whole is as important as its parts.

Let us consider a 'simple' example – the use of an online customer relationship management (CRM) application to manage sales information, which is accessible from a variety of user devices, including employees' own smartphones. As soon as security questions start to be asked (such as 'How is the customer information protected against threats?') the example becomes a lot less simple: answering the question requires taking a wealth of issues into account, including:

- how trusted is the online hosting provider;
- whether the sales person's smartphone has a security code enabled;
- or, whether it can be accessed by family members.

Indeed, as Figure 1.1 illustrates, customer data can be in any one of a diverse range of places. None of these issues can be resolved simply, which demonstrates just how complex information security has become.

Figure 1.1 Customer data can exist across a variety of locations

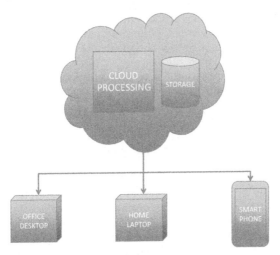

One option, of course, is to stop employees from using their own devices, but this needs to be weighed against the corporate advantage gained from allowing them to be used. Equally, will users of the CRM and other systems (considering that we are talking about everybody, from the receptionist to the chief executive) pay any attention to such edicts? Even if they do, focusing on the technology is a relentless task – new devices and services are released all the time, often rendering past policy statements redundant.

Equally clearly, it does not make sense to address any one element of the above example, without assuring the rest is secured to the same level. It is an old security adage that a chain is only as strong as its weakest link; the difference today is that we are dealing with chain-link fences, rather than single strands. Treating security requires considering the mesh of technologies and information sources as a whole, and deploying security controls – technical mechanisms as well as policies and procedures – at appropriate points.

Given such a broad remit, those tasked with delivering the security architecture for an organisation must be technology experts as well as proponents of change, able to drive beneficial security improvements across the business through the deployment or review of security controls which:

- take into account the IT environment as a whole, rather than on a piecemeal basis;
- fit business requirements for security, in terms of strategy, policy and process;
- balance information risk against the cost of any countermeasures.

Security architects need not only to be up to date with the latest technologies and how they integrate and interact, but also to understand business models and risks, governance and compliance requirements, employee behaviours and expectations, the relationships with partners and consumers – the list goes on. In some cases, this will require hard choices. The security architect's role is not simply that of technician and enforcer, but also educator and facilitator, sometimes working at the highest levels of the organisation.

THE AIM OF THIS BOOK

This book seeks to help those interested in security architecture understand its founding principles and essence, as well as the skills and expertise security architects should bring to bear, and how to adopt the right spirit in what can be a complex and challenging environment. While examples are included, the need to understand the underlying principles is far more important than remembering the examples.

While this book is aimed at anyone with an interest in this field, to fully benefit, readers will gain from having a reasonable grounding in IT and general information security. As security architecture captures the security aspects of more general IT architecture topics, an understanding of what is meant by architecture in the enterprise context, across concepts and practice, can certainly help. A short introduction to these areas is provided in the text.

The book does not provide examples in any technical depth, nor does it go into detail about information security practices. Additional guidance is available from the references and further reading sections at the end of the book.

While readers are likely to be involved in the design, definition or review of security strategy, policy, or practice, or the specification, deployment or operation of technical security controls, these are not essential prerequisites. Some reference literature around information security and assurance can be long-winded and dry, so above all, this book aims to be both readable and informative.

CAVEATS

Terminology can be a difficult area, particularly in security circles. For example, the term 'security control' is defined by some sources to mean a general statement about a security requirement ('all backups must be encrypted') whereas others define it to mean a specific mechanism ('backup encryption'). The term can also be domain-specific, for example the activities conducted by airport security are also called security controls. Equally, an organisation may have its own views on or traditions governing how terms are used. So, the priority for someone looking to apply the principles in this book is to define terms for their own organisation and be consistent in their use. Where possible, ISO definitions are used in this book; a glossary of terms is provided.

The terms 'data' and 'information' are used interchangeably. While it is understood that in other contexts, information is seen as a refined form of data, in security risk management terms the needs are usually the same for both. So, for example, 'data security' and 'information security' are synonymous for the purposes of security architecture. Equally, while the term 'information assurance' is described in Chapter 2, the term 'information security' is adopted when talking about general aspects in this book. The term 'information technology' is used in preference to (the more clunky) 'information and communications technology'.

While this book references a number of other disciplines, notably enterprise architecture and enterprise management, it does not cover these in any detail. For enterprise architecture I recommend The Open Group Architectural Framework (TOGAF) and for enterprise management the Information Technology Infrastructure Library (ITIL) and Control Objectives for Information and related Technology (COBIT).

For retailers and their financial partners, the current Payment Card Industry – Data Security Standard (PCI-DSS) offers a good source of information on compliance practices these sectors are required to meet, to process any form of payment cards. In addition, the Information Commissioner's Office provides useful information on the protection and processing of personal data. References to all of the above are provided in the references and further reading sections at the end of the book.

Finally, while national and international standards have been referenced throughout the book, it has been written in the UK, based primarily on UK law. Practitioners should have an awareness of the standards and regulations that apply to their own sectors and geographies.

2 INFORMATION SECURITY ARCHITECTURE FUNDAMENTALS

Newcomers to the field of information security may wonder where on earth to start, given the rapidly shifting technological landscape that exists today. Even over the past decade, IT has moved from being an arm's-length set of capabilities – as corporate systems, mostly accessed via fixed desktops – to becoming an intrinsic part of everything that the business, its employees and customers do.

The good news is that we do have a starting point, which is to remember what we are trying to secure – not technology for its own sake, but the information it processes and transmits. In this chapter we review some of the areas that are making information security so challenging. We then look at the essentials of information security in the context of the modern organisation, to see how and where security architecture needs to respond.

INFORMATION SECURITY IN A CHANGING WORLD

The latest waves of information technology have profoundly affected business and economic models across all sectors and geographies, and are having a significant impact on the nature of business risk. Just a few years ago, for example, email was seen as relatively new and a major target for attack; then came instant messaging systems, open to malicious communications and offering the potential for fraud; shortly after that, Voice over Internet Protocol mechanisms such as Skype were considered to be high-risk and needing to be treated with some urgency.

Each generation of technology has been seen to constitute a major threat when it emerged, and no doubt each still does. However, just as past technologies have been superseded, so more recent developments are creating new opportunities for both the malicious and the stupid to do harm:

Teleworking is becoming the default way of working, rather than the exception, for large numbers of staff at many organisations. This has a highly disruptive impact on the notion of physical protection. For example, traditionally the idea of securing 'on-site' versus 'off-site' equipment made sense; today, however, two staff members may meet in a café to exchange information using a non-corporate-issue USB stick. Security managers can quickly become unstuck if they treat remote workers and equipment in the same way as office-based, corporate IT.

Mobile devices, smartphones and tablets are rapidly overtaking desktop computers as end-user computing devices, changing the way people interact with online and corporate services. While they enable people to work more flexibly, they are also easier to steal or lose. An added complication is the fact that people are increasingly using their own devices at work – so-called 'bring your own device' (BYOD). New device capabilities are causing new issues – for example cyber-bullying via photo apps such as Snapchat, or the use of encrypted messaging such as Blackberry Messenger, which was used during the riots of 2011.

Payment cards and associated information have emerged as a significant area of concern for IT security professionals. Such is the significance of payment card data that the major card providers have established an independent organisation, the PCI-DSS Council, to deliver a fully regulated model which defines mechanisms and practices for its protection. This requires organisations to employ independent accredited approved security vendors and their employed qualified security assessors to assess and certify in-scope payment card data environments in accordance with PCI-DSS Council rules.

Public cloud computing involves the delivery of scalable IT services running on hosted servers and using the internet as transport. Benefits are variously cited as scalability, cost-effectiveness and ease of deployment. However, security ramifications include dependency on (potentially untrusted) third parties, location sensitivity and increased potential for surveillance, as well as consumerisation-linked risk from individuals subscribing to services themselves. Cloud computing models are also diversifying – for example, hosting and co-location companies are now offering hybrid models such as 'private hosted cloud'.

Social networking builds on the public cloud, enabling people to interact, collaborate and share information using publicly available, free-to-use services such as Google, Twitter and Facebook. Many corporate, entertainment and sport websites also build in a social element. As a result customers can have more direct relations with organisations; the downside is that they may also complain, loudly and globally. Some social sites have been criticised for failing to protect the privacy of their users – as the adage goes, 'If the service is free, you are the product.' Hackers are also known to trawl social networks for personal information that can be used for targeted email attacks.

Data centre virtualisation is where computer servers run multiple workloads using software to emulate a physical computer. Today's top-end servers can run tens of 'virtual' machines. While these can be relocated relatively easily, they have to be secured as individual computers. In addition, they rely on a virtual machine management console, which is often seen as the weakest link from a security perspective – a username/password breach can deliver access to the entire estate of virtual machines. Third-party software suites that deliver management information for virtualised environments also create a significant attack surface for hackers.

Broadband and mobile networking make it easier to work from home or on the move. While higher-bandwidth connections tend to be restricted to municipal areas (which is as much a problem for itinerant workers as those living in rural areas), the level of available bandwidth continues to increase, driving the demand for remote working. Note that the latest 4G mobile technologies operate more quickly than Wi-Fi, potentially driving people towards using their own, potentially less secure mobile devices, connected to less trusted networks, for data transfers and communications. Access control and authentication, end-point security, and the protection of corporate data across multiple devices will continue to deliver complex challenges for the IT security professional.

Big data analytics relies on the continuing phenomenon of Moore's law – that the number of transistors on a chip will double every 18 months. Just as data volumes are expanding as we become able to generate data in greater and greater quantities, so the ways in which data can be stored and analysed are expanding, for example using analytics platforms such as Hadoop. However, such technologies also create new opportunities for hackers, not least because greater volumes of data need to be protected; equally, privacy concerns exist around the ability to identify individuals from analysis of aggregated data.

The Internet of Things (also known as machine-to-machine communications) presents another manifestation of Moore's law, in that as processors become cheaper and more powerful, it becomes possible to connect an increasing range of devices to the internet. This creates new possibilities – for example, smarter buildings and cars – but also creates a new set of security risks. Not least among these is the protection of connected equipment and generated data; for example, the Stuxnet computer worm was designed to attack industrial control systems running the Supervisory Control and Data Acquisition (SCADA) protocol. Equally, the internet of things raises a number of potential privacy concerns, illustrated by the case of London bins being used to track passers-by, via their mobile phone signatures.

Trends such as these are leading to new ways in which governments, corporations and individuals procure, design and use computer systems and services. In 2012, for example, the UK Cabinet Office announced the G-Cloud initiative, 'developed to give customers access to pay-as-you-go services as a cheaper alternative to traditionally sourced ICT'.[1] For providers, cloud computing is also leading to new system architecture approaches – as illustrated by NoSQL databases or the 'built to fail, but gracefully' design principles of online services such as Netflix.

Simultaneously, these trends create opportunities for malicious individuals and organisations to breach corporate security and put businesses at risk, with potentially expensive consequences. Hacker groups may target both businesses and customers with attacks with names such as 'man in the middle' and 'watering hole', exploiting weaknesses across the evolving technology ecosystem. Equally, employees may foolishly seek to find out colleagues' salaries, or inadvertently lose corporate information; in 2012, for example, Greater Manchester Police was fined £120,000 for the loss of a USB stick containing data about people linked to serious crime, which was stolen from the house of a police officer. Just as technology continues to diversify, so do the number of ways things can go wrong.

OVERVIEW OF INFORMATION SECURITY CONCEPTS

How can traditional security stand a chance of responding to such challenges? A generally accepted principle of technology-related security, which remains valid even through such change, is that the 'core asset' at the heart of what we want to secure is information. Other types of security exist, of course – such as physical security to protect buildings and working environments, which we reference in Chapter 4. However, just as information technology exists to enable the creation, processing, communication and storage of information, so information security exists to protect **information assets** against **threats** by limiting their **vulnerabilities and** reducing **risks.**

---

[1] http://gcloud.civilservice.gov.uk/about/

Figure 2.1 Information security provides a protective layer against external attacks

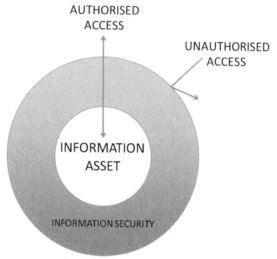

As shown in Figure 2.1, information security provides a protective layer that allows authorised access to information assets while preventing unauthorised access. Information assets constitute any items of information that are seen as having value to the organisation. Size is unimportant, as the following examples show:

- A paint manufacturer has a master list of discounts offered to each of its major customers, stored as a simple office document, such as a word-processing file or spreadsheet. Disclosure could result in different customers seeking renegotiation of their own discounts, and the document may be a target of industrial espionage.

- A hospital system holds the personal details of a famous actor who has just been admitted for unexpected surgery. Junior clinical staff may find it difficult to overcome the temptation of calling the press and receiving payment for the 'scoop'.

- An industrial machine is connected to the internet for monitoring purposes, using the SCADA protocol. In this case, the risk is that it can inadvertently be controlled or compromised by the actions of a third party, which could damage the machine or compromise the process it serves.

- A retail organisation stores customer payment card information unencrypted, and is hacked. Resulting fines amount to a significant percentage of the organisation's annual turnover, and the damage to its brand is enough to push the organisation into administration.

In such cases as these, the potential outcome of a security breach (the **impact**) could come with a price tag greater than the information suggests. An organisation can lose money directly – through the costs of resolving a breach, responding to customer calls or lost sales – or indirectly – for example, dealing with litigation or repairing reputational damage. In some cases, the cost of a breach can be many times that of the mechanisms that could have been implemented to avoid it, a fact that security vendors are often keen to emphasise.

In today's distributed and communications-rich context, we need to think about protecting not only the information, but also the services and transmission mechanisms we use to operate and access it. This means recognising two kinds of information:

- **information at rest** – stored on a server, desktop computer, mobile phone, USB stick or other device;
- **information in transit** – being transmitted across a fixed or wireless network.

Let us be clear, however - it is information, not technology, that we are ultimately looking to protect. Nobody really cares about whether a system or communications mechanism is secure in its own right; far more important is whether the information it contains or transmits is at risk. While this may sound self-evident, it is not always the way that security is discussed – a conversation may refer to securing a database rather than the data, for example.

Information assurance

The need to address concerns around more tactical approaches to information security led to the creation of a new discipline – of information assurance, first defined in 2002 by the US Department of Defense (DoD). The original definition has been updated by the UK CESG and Office of Cyber Security and Information Assurance, as follows:

'Information Assurance is the confidence that information systems will protect the information they handle and will function as they need to, when they need to, under the control of legitimate users.'[2]

In other words, the original field of information security – which has been defined around protecting data assets – has expanded to what is a very broad field indeed – based around a more general term of 'confidence'.

What do we mean by protection? According to international standard definitions such as those documented in ISO 13335,[3] themselves derived from years of practical security experience, information risks, and therefore the protections we might want to put in place, respond to three core attributes that the information needs to maintain:

---

[2] https://www.gov.uk/government/policy-teams/office-of-cyber-security-and-information-assurance

[3] We follow the General Information Assurance Products and Services Initiative definitions, as described in the Appendix.

- **Confidentiality** – the property that information is not made available or disclosed to unauthorised individuals, entities or processes.

- **Integrity** – the property of safeguarding the accuracy and completeness of assets.

- **Availability** - the property of being accessible and usable upon demand by an authorised entity.

Other standards incorporate more nuanced definitions – for example, the European Network and Information Security Agency defines integrity as 'The protection of communications or stored data against interception and reading by unauthorised persons'. Fundamentally, however, the three needs – to keep information confidential, uncorrupted and available – remain firmly at the centre of good security practice.

While this should come as some relief to anybody considering how to address the security concerns of today, the task has clearly become harder than it used to be. A few decades ago, addressing confidentiality, integrity and availability largely meant considering isolated systems and whether they could be 'penetrated'. As we have already noted, the notion of individual systems has largely been replaced by a disparate, complex array of technologies and services.

Ensuring an appropriate level of security protection requires the deployment of technological and procedural security mechanisms – known as **security controls** – across the IT environment. Information security controls include:[4]

- access controls and authentication mechanisms;

- cryptographic tools;

- firewalls and virtual private network (VPN) equipment;

- anti-malware protection (against viruses, trojans, for example);

- operational policies, procedures and processes.

---

[4] Further examples can be found at http://www.sans.org/critical-security-controls/

Security controls make use of **security features** – that is, capabilities that enable data or processes to be protected. Of all security features, the most important are encryption and authentication – which we consider in Chapter 3. As discussed, however, system-specific, piecemeal approaches are generally recognised as insufficient to mitigate the kinds of risks inherent in the modern enterprise IT environment.

To respond to this challenge, we can draw on another fundamental principle of information security – **defence in depth**, which refers to taking a layered approach to information security. The simplest view of defence in depth is as a series of concentric circles, also referred to as tiers (Figure 2.2). The outermost can be the least secure, containing the least valuable information; at the core are the organisation's most valuable information assets, accessible only to those with the highest levels of clearance. Each circle represents a layer of protection – just like an old fortress, complete with outer wall, inner wall and keep.

Figure 2.2 Defence in depth implies a multi-layered approach to protecting security assets

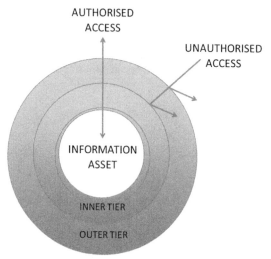

The core notions of security architecture extend the principles of defence in depth and tiering. In the earlier days of computing, the concentric circle idea worked well – for example, a decade or so ago we would talk about intranet, extranet and internet as valid tiers. An additional implication was that the chief security officer held the keys to the entire 'fortress'.

However, to secure today's highly distributed computing models, incorporating cloud computing, virtualisation and mobile networks, we require a number of additional concepts:

- **Security domains** group together elements of technology that need to be secured in a similar way (Figure 2.3). These can be physical – for example, the corporate LAN or the data centre may be seen as a specific security domain. Equally, they can be logical – finance and human resources (HR) systems, or specific information assets requiring similar levels or protection, for example, can be grouped into the same security domain.

- **Domains** can be used not just for security but also efficiency and manageability. For example, payment card data domains are often segregated from other corporate domains so that only the card data domain is within the scope of PCI-DSS compliance assessment and certification. Should any changes be required, only the domain needs to be re-audited, not the entire IT environment.

- **Trust levels** provide an indication of the relationship between security domains. So, for example, a publicly accessible security domain (containing corporate web servers) may be considered as less trusted than a security domain for internal systems, meaning that one cannot automatically be accessed from the other.

Figure 2.3 Security domains group technology elements that need to be secured in a similar way

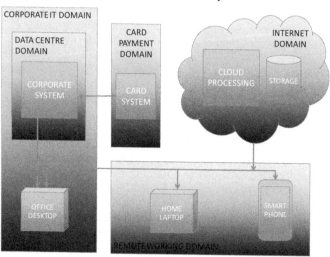

Not only do security domains – which we discuss in more detail in Chapter 3 – put boundaries around areas of the IT environment. They also enable us to describe constraints to be imposed on administrators and users, for example in terms of:

- **Security policies** – defining which actors (people, systems or roles) are able to access information assets in a given security domain, according to specific rules.

- **Separation of duties** – no one individual should have access to all the systems in an organisation, or indeed potentially all the configuration data for a single system. The person could be corrupted in some way, or do accidental damage or simply leave without sharing the knowledge.

- **Least privilege** – this refers to allocation of access rights in terms of only those rights necessary to do the job in hand. For example, this means enabling read-only access for system monitoring while not allowing for configuration changes or information access, or ensuring that certain parts of the source code are accessible only by select groups of developers on a need-to-access basis.

We shall build on these concepts throughout this book.

THE ROLE OF IT AND ENTERPRISE ARCHITECTURE IN INFORMATION SECURITY

Information technology architecture is a well-established discipline covering the specification, design, development and deployment of computer systems and services. However, as technology options and business requirements have evolved over the years, it has become increasingly difficult to consider any single technical capability in isolation from its business context. In response, the field of enterprise architecture has been established, embracing every aspect of the business and how it uses technology.

Enterprise architecture starts right at the top of the organisation, using the strategic goals of the business as a basis to understand its information needs, as specified by its:

- **Vision** – a high-level statement about the impact the organisation wants to have, for example, 'to work towards a world where people can deliver on their potential';

- **Mission** – a statement about what the organisation is hoping to achieve, for example, 'to become the world number one manufacturer of widgets';

- **Objectives** – statements about the priority goals of the organisation, for example, 'to grow through acquisition' and 'optimise supply chain processes'.

Enterprise architecture offers a number of mechanisms to enable the modelling and analysis of the business and its technology needs. As well as recognising that a company's IT should reflect its business goals, it takes the broadest possible definition of scope: if something is within the scope of the organisation, then it should be covered by the enterprise architecture.

As such, enterprise architecture provides us with an appropriate starting point for understanding both IT strategy and IT architecture. According to the definitions of enterprise architecture, IT strategy is required to deliver tangible, measurable results and not just loose aspirations about how IT will deliver 'great things'. Tangibility can be achieved, for example, by prioritising objectives, creating a roadmap for when goals will be delivered, analysing financial benefits and so on.

The same principle applies to information security strategy – it is all very well saying the organisation should be secure, but a clear roadmap makes objectives more likely to be achieved. While this is not the place to go into detail about IT or information security strategy (see Taylor et al. 2013), as shown in Figure 2.4, we can take into account that:

- business strategy yields both enterprise architecture and enterprise security policy;
- enterprise architecture then begets IT architecture;
- IT architecture works with IT security strategy to deliver the information security architecture.

A number of enterprise architecture frameworks exist, including TOGAF and the Zachmann framework for enterprise. Created to support the certification of enterprise architects, the BCS Reference Model in Enterprise and Solution Architecture (BCS 2012) incorporates elements of these frameworks and provides us with a number of relevant definitions. As we discuss in Chapter 4, anyone working with enterprise and IT architects (not least, security architects) will need to be able to talk the same language, so it is a valuable skill to understand and use terms such as:

Figure 2.4 Information security architecture derives from IT architecture and information security strategy

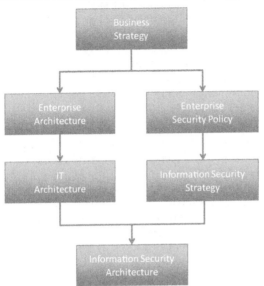

- **System** – A structure of interacting subsystems or components that perform activities, or an encapsulated collection of processes that transform inputs into outputs. From an architect's perspective, this will normally refer to one or more server computers running a software package – say, SAP installed on an HP server. At the highest level, the term can refer to the entire business – for example, the UK railway system.

- **Service** – The outcome of a process that is executed in response to a request from a client. Architects are generally more interested in services than systems. For example, the email service requires a number of systems to be in place, including the email server, gateways and clients (as well as the hardware they run upon). Similarly, SAP may be considered as a system, providing a number of services.

- **Process** – A procedure, started by an event, which terminates with the delivery of an output or service. The most important type of process for an enterprise architect is a business process, responding to a business event (for example, a customer request). Systems also have processes, but these can be seen as responding to system requests triggered by business processes.

- **Component** – A subsystem encapsulated behind an interface, so it can be replaced by any other with the same interface. In general, components provide the building blocks for systems. Architects look for 'well-bounded' components, which have minimal dependencies with other components and which perform a coherent set of functions well. Components manage specific information elements, which can be accessed via services offered by the component's one or more interfaces.

- **Interface** – The means of connecting to a system, process or component; usually via a list of services, offered by one or more components. As interfaces provide connection points between systems and components, they are important to get right from the perspective of architecture. In general, architects look to minimise dependencies between systems, processes and components, as these add overheads of both time and cost.

Just as IT strategy needs to reflect business strategy, so information security principles, when presented at the highest level, need to reflect the organisation's strategic goals. Information security starts with the corporate or **enterprise security policy** – an über-policy that sets the company's security stance and expectations for staff. At this level the principles may be quite generic – 'the security of customer data is paramount,' for example.

Creating an enterprise security policy is outside the scope of this book. However, it stands to reason that the enterprise security policy is more likely to be adopted if it is endorsed by the board, aligned with corporate strategy and communicated throughout the organisation – so it must above all be practical and achievable. Derived from the enterprise security policy, the IT security strategy lays out the objectives to be achieved by deployment of security processes and controls. With the IT security strategy in place, the goal of security architecture becomes that of delivering on the requirements it specifies.

INTRODUCING INFORMATION SECURITY ARCHITECTURE

So far we have confirmed how the core principles of information security remain valid, despite the technological landscape having changed unrecognisably (and continuing to evolve). We have also noted that security needs to be considered across the entire IT environment, reducing information risks wherever that information resides, rather than looking at systems in isolation. Finally, we have looked at the growing importance of architecture in both understanding the business and designing appropriate technology solutions, particularly in the context of larger, more complex organisations.

Thus we have a backdrop for how to protect information and minimise business risks from the perspective of the entire IT architecture. At its highest level, the purpose of security architecture is to deliver on the requirements expressed in the security strategy through the appropriate use of security controls, in order to mitigate any security risks and protect the information assets of the organisation. We have already seen how this ties in smoothly with the core security principles of confidentiality, integrity and availability.

Delivering on these goals requires the skilled application of security mechanisms and controls across the broad environment of IT-related systems and services. Security architecture is not something you can simply buy off the shelf, for a number of reasons: first, no two IT environments are the same; second, no two security strategies are the same, as different companies have different business models and attitudes to risk; third, the regulatory compliance conditions and governance constraints may be different; and finally, every business and every IT environment is in a constant state of change.

So, how precisely should a security architecture be created for a given organisation? In layman's terms, the 'recipe' is as follows:

- Take one IT architecture.

- Review the security needs of the business and the risks it faces.

- Identify the applicable regulatory compliance controls.

- In response, identify an appropriate set of security controls.

- Deploy these at appropriate points in the IT architecture.

While this risks oversimplifying the whole thing (we present a more formal process in Chapter 3), it serves to demonstrate that the security architecture does not exist in isolation from the IT architecture. Rather, the former is more of an overlay on the latter, tightening the controls at appropriate points to ensure the security of the environment as a whole. For a more formal starting point, we need look no further than the reference model for the BCS Certificates in Enterprise and Solution Architecture (BCS 2012), which defines security architecture as: 'The various design features to protect a system from unauthorised access.' The factors we have already described would suggest extending the definition to encompass the notion of an end-to-end service, and the fact that it is, ultimately, the information that we are trying to protect, giving us: 'The various design features, applied to a system or service, to protect information from breaches of confidentiality, integrity or availability.' In general this will result in the implementation of security controls within, and at integration points between, security domains. Example control points are illustrated in Figure 2.5.

Figure 2.5 Security control points exist at the boundaries of security domains

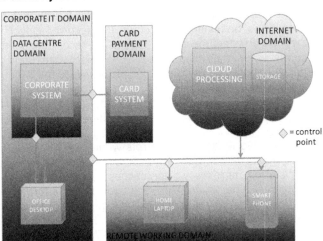

As well as conforming with the corporate security strategy or enterprise security policy, security architecture needs to take into account other areas of business and IT governance and practice, as represented by:

- corporate policies and how they map onto business processes and activities;

- procedures in terms of how systems are to be managed, administered and operated;

- user behaviours, for example in terms of acceptable use of systems and services.

Security architecture provides a **common and consistent** set of security controls to apply across the organisation, across all systems, locations and users. At its heart lies a high-level, logical design exercise, the results of which can be taken into account by system implementers. For example, the security architecture may specify that a certain network connection needs to be encrypted; it does not, however, need to detail the products or services used.

Can the security architecture inform the IT architecture? Indeed it can, by taking into account the security aspects of different IT architecture options and making recommendations accordingly. A simple example is the choice between running a service in-house and using a hosted facility. While the in-house system might benefit (in security terms) from being situated behind the corporate firewall, a hosted data centre may offer resilience advantages over in-house facilities.

In an ideal world, security controls would be defined at the same time as a system's features and functions. As The Open Group states: 'There are two approaches to developing a secure architecture: the "build-it-in" and "bolt-it-on" approaches.' Security professionals know that it is far more effective to build in security requirements and relevant controls early in the development of a system or service. We call this 'security by design' – that is, organisations benefit from considering how to meet security needs in advance and apply appropriate technical solutions before problems occur, rather than picking up the pieces after the event.

It is not always possible to build in security by design, however: as the technology environment changes, new vulnerabilities emerge, as recent examples illustrate – employees wanting to access email on their personal devices, or companies requiring previously unconnected devices and physical objects (from healthcare equipment to air conditioning systems) to be managed remotely and/or centrally.

Security architecture can be likened to fixing new windscreens on a moving train – while not impossible, it is far from ideal.

IT security often finds itself the poor nephew of more general IT implementation, for a number of reasons. It can be treated as second priority to getting basic functionality right – 'Let's build the app, then we'll think about how to secure it'. Equally, it can be perceived by managers as a bureaucratic overhead which does not contribute to the success of the business. Often, technology architecture decisions are already in place and then need to be reviewed to build in security.

As such, we need to consider how security architecture principles can be applied to a pre-existing environment. Let's be under no illusion – this is not always going to be easy to achieve. We shall look into the activities and processes around the development of the security architecture in Chapter 3.

THE ROLE OF THE BUSINESS IN THE SECURITY ARCHITECTURE

Given the strategic nature of security architecture, it makes absolute sense that the business should have input concerning the measures and controls to be implemented. In an ideal world, this would involve a dialogue between the security architect and a representative of the business as a whole, or an individual department, at the most senior level possible. The result (one would hope) would be a clear, transparent and honest discussion about:

- risks that genuinely exist to the business;
- information assets, systems and services to be protected;
- the potential impact of a breach on the wider business;
- security controls that would be appropriate in response;
- training and awareness requirements for staff.

We shall pick up on these points in Chapter 3. Note that such a dialogue cannot be considered as a fait accompli, to be embraced wholeheartedly by every management team or head of department. Different organisations can have very different attitudes to risk – with some playing fast and loose with confidential information, and others wanting to protect it with a 'belt and braces' approach.

Neither model is necessarily incorrect from a business perspective; rather it is a question for the company board to answer, based on its chosen business model, its regulatory environment and local, national and international law. Organisations do not always get this right: in recent years we have seen numerous failures of corporate governance, from Enron and WorldCom in the early 2000s, to the sub-prime banking crisis and interest rate fixing scandals of more recent years. It is fair to say that business executives involved in fraud might not be too interested in the minutiae of information security.

Even for tightly run, ethically sound organisations, information security can have a reputation for getting in the way of good business. Security controls can be awkward or bureaucratic, with a perceived or real negative impact on productivity, if they are not designed with people in mind. For example, a remote worker might not be able to access the VPN or could be otherwise slowed down. In one example, UK office staff were told to store office documents on a file share situated in New York, for security reasons – the result was that larger spreadsheets took painful minutes to open or save.

Controls can also become quite obtrusive or invasive for individuals. For example, mechanisms now exist to log personnel movements and locations, or to perform facial recognition of customers entering stores. Organisations have a duty of care towards employees, contractors and customers, which needs to be taken into account as security controls are deployed.

Finally, across many sectors the business landscape is changing as quickly as the IT environment, due to global economics, demographic shifts and, indeed, the impact of technology. Given that business and IT, and therefore enterprise and IT architecture, are evolving so fast, they cannot be hampered by onerous or inflexible guidance, which is more likely to be ignored as a result. Indeed, it will be all security architecture can do to keep up.

The bottom line is, while information security professionals used to consider the IT environment as a fortress to be shored up, with security acting as gatekeeper, in today's world security and the business need a more interactive, constructive dialogue which considers how security can help the business move forward, rather than simply imposing controls and policy rules without consultation. As Hugh Thompson, Chief Security Strategist at security vendor Blue Coat Systems, Inc., said: 'Security is not just about what you prevent, it's about what you make possible.'

3 INFORMATION SECURITY ARCHITECTURE ACTIVITIES

Given that the security architecture augments the outputs of information assurance, enterprise architecture, systems and software design, development and so on, it makes sense that no standard definition exists for a security architecture life cycle. Rather, security architecture activities need to align to the life cycles and working practices of these and other disciplines.

All the same, the process of taking an organisation from a 'non-security-architected' to a 'security-architected' state can benefit from a level of formalisation (and indeed, does follow a life cycle of sorts). The stages of process enable the architect to gain an understanding of the problem space, define appropriate security enhancements and oversee their deployment, for example, as follows:

- **Collation** – collection of materials from a range of sources, to be used as input to the security architecture.

- **Scoping** – identification of areas that the security architecture needs to prioritise, treat or exclude.

- **Threat and vulnerability assessment** – review of existing and planned business and technology capabilities and associated risks.

- **Assessment of existing controls** – review of known and potential issues stemming from existing security controls.

- **Domain definition** – identification of areas sharing security requirements, and their relative trust levels.

- **Specification of controls** – recommendation of technical mechanisms to strengthen security within and between domains.
- **Evaluation of options** – define mechanisms to eliminate, reduce or transfer the risks, or decide to accept them.
- **Business case** – creation of a costed proposal that a business or technology budget holder can sign off.
- **Implementation** – overseeing the deployment of security controls across the IT environment.
- **Monitoring and review** – post-deployment, maintaining a view on emerging threats and the continued suitability of the architecture.

While we expand upon these stages[1] below, note that in practice it would not be possible for the security architect to undertake all of the activities described here, even if capable – it would simply take too long. Instead the role is one of expert mentor and guide, collating information and facilitating whichever activities are required to collate information as a basis for making recommendations, which the architect then presents in such a way as to maximise the chances of deployment.

Successful completion of the 'security architecture life cycle' depends therefore on stakeholders who are fully engaged with the process and who have sufficient interest, muscle and, indeed, budget to ensure it delivers. To this end it is useful to invoke, request the services of, or even form a security architecture steering group, the role of which is to:

- review the output of each stage;
- confirm its objectives are being achieved;

---

[1] Note that the activities described here do not map directly onto the syllabus areas of Senior IA Architect (SFIA Level 6), IISP Skill Level 2/3, not least because some topics expressed in these syllabuses are quite specific (for example, 'establishes training programmes for security architects') whereas others are more generic (for example, 'recognise security as a business enabler').

- gain or increase the buy-in from business units;
- ensure involvement of internal and external assessors.

A suitable group may exist already; if not, it probably should be formed – creating this might be the security architect's first challenge!

COLLATION

Where does security architecture start, in practical terms? It is unlikely (and it would be unfair in the extreme) for security architects to find themselves 'parachuted' into a business environment with no pre-existing status of IT architecture or information security. Nonetheless it is worth the security architect starting as if operating with a blank canvas, upon which a realistic picture – figuratively or graphically – of the organisation's existing IT environment, security strategy and controls in place, can be drawn.

As collation begins, the security architect is likely to be in one of three situations. There may be a company-wide activity to implement security architecture where one did not exist before or where existing controls across the IT environment were piecemeal and out of date. Alternatively, the security architect may be brought in to assess the architectural aspects of a new solution or service, in which case the scope will be more limited (though an understanding of the existing IT environment and security architecture will be required). Finally, a change in the regulatory compliance criteria against which the corporate IT environment is assessed might need the architect to recommend changes.

Given that we are most interested in information security, it makes sense that any collation activities are focused on business data, who should have access to it, where and how it is stored, and how it is transported within and across systems and services. To build such a picture, the security architect needs to be able to pull together information from across business and IT departments, based on several sources:

- **Business requirements and models** – that is, the way that the business operates and, therefore, the organisation's information and service requirements, as well as working practices on the ground.

- **Enterprise and IT architecture, system and service information** – services seen as business-critical may be documented in the form of service level agreements (SLAs).

- **Systems requirements and plans** – technical documentation concerning existing systems, as well as the 'roadmap' presented in the organisation's IT strategy.

- **Information asset registers** – information can be classified (protectively marked) according to the governance criteria that apply to them, and the impact should anything happen.

- **Contracts with service providers and subcontractors** – these provide information about services being procured from outside, including cloud-based services.

- **Locations where information is stored** – including off-site backups and personal phones, as well as transits including networks, and physical transfers including transport to disposal facilities.

- **Corporate, IT and security strategy documents** – including organisational security roles and responsibilities (see below) and existing policies, procedures and guidelines (Chapter 4).

- **Risk assessments or risk registers** – which document potential threats to the business. These may have been created as part of security, business continuity or disaster recovery documentation.

- **Existing security architecture documentation** – for example, if working for a subsidiary of a larger company which already has a security architecture in place.

- **Interviews with key staff** – for example, heads of department, operations personnel and others likely to require access to more sensitive information.

- **Regulatory compliance documentation** – applicable regulatory, audit, and compliance controls and their relevance to which parts of the business.

- **Corporate and external audit groups** – which carry out commercial and regulatory audit activities as a business deliverable.

If the business, IT or existing security management is not able to furnish the above information at a sufficient level to define a security architecture, then this is a major risk in itself (equivalent to flying an aeroplane with no real knowledge of whether it can stay in the air) and should be flagged as such, in no uncertain terms. 'I'm sorry, but the way that things are at the moment, it is very difficult to create a comprehensive security architecture' is a difficult thing to say at the best of times. At such moments, the security architect may come to understand exactly why they require communication skills.

SCOPING

Once the above information has been collated, the security architect needs to consider scope – that is, what areas of the business and IT environment are to be included and, just as importantly, excluded. In principle, there is little that does not have the potential to be part of the security architecture. Many systems and services are interdependent, relying on the same infrastructure and end-point devices. Equally, neither vulnerabilities nor hackers care about whether a piece of computer equipment is corporate issue or a personal acquisition, nor how or where it is being used.

As a result, even if the security architecture exercise is taking place as part of the delivery of a specific solution, it still needs to take the broader IT environment into account. In many organisations this can be extremely complicated, running across many offices, data centres and the wider internet, and changing dynamically every day. Clearly, corporate security cannot enforce stringent controls across every element of the IT environment – and nor does it need to: for example, low-risk information, such as that already visible on the website, does not require to be managed as carefully as customer data or partner price lists.

Figure 3.1, from online data collation and correlation company DataSift, illustrates how complex IT architectures can become; for many organisations such a diagram represents only the tip of the iceberg!

Figure 3.1 IT architectures can become quite complex!
Please refer to http://from.io/complexarch for a slightly different, but more legible version of this figure.

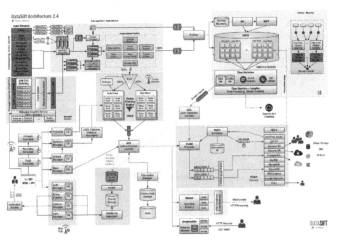

Scoping the security architecture therefore needs to set a realistic goal for what needs to be secured. While you can fix scope according to geography or corporate structure, the best scoping approach by far is in terms of the list of technology-based **services** being delivered, and the **information assets** they handle. What do we mean by technology-based services? As discussed in Chapter 2, a service generates an outcome in response to a client request – for example, 'email', 'HR' or 'CRM'. A list of services may be documented as part of the organisation's IT architecture. Note that a service may encompass several systems; for example, a hosted CRM service involves the hosted software provided via the internet, local and remote desktops, and mobile devices – all of which may have security weaknesses.

As this suggests, it is not just corporate systems and officially sourced services that should be included as candidates to be in the scope of the security architecture. For example, it might be a common practice for employees to use hosted storage or private email to send large files, or to deliver presentations to clients and prospects using a tablet computer. Not only does the volume and variety of technologies at play make it difficult to enforce a separation of concerns between corporate and personal use, but also IT security practitioners rightly recognise that technology elements outside corporate control present additional security risks. For example:

- Personal computers are notorious breeding grounds for 'malware' – a general label for such infections as trojans, viruses and so on. These issues can often be caused by browsing poorly secured websites.

- Home equipment may be used by multiple people, including children and friends; USB sticks can be lent to a neighbour to exchange photos or documents, and can pick up viruses as a result.

- Mobile devices are very easy to steal or lose, and (depending on the configuration) may store email attachments on an easily removable memory card.

From the security architect's perspective, therefore, what people are **actually** using is more important than what they **should** be using. The security architecture needs to cover all technologies involved in the processing of corporate information – wherever they are, and to whomever they belong. If a smartphone contains corporate data, then it is in scope. However, we also need to recognise that it is not possible to 'sheep-dip' every USB stick, every smartphone or every computer browser likely to come into contact with corporate information (even if using an appropriately scoped and fully operational mobile device management solution).

As a result, security architects are most concerned about services and information assets deemed to be 'business-critical', as documented in system requirements, asset registers and so on. Information can be said to be business-critical if a breach of its confidentiality, availability or integrity is seen as sufficiently damaging to the organisation, for example in terms of whether it can continue to function, or resulting financial or reputational costs. If a business-critical information asset is in scope, then so are all of the services, systems and devices that might handle it.

The security architect's job can be greatly simplified if some kind of information classification or protective marking scheme is in place. Protective marking schemes classify documents and files according to clearly defined labels based on:

- **the information itself** – such as secret, commercial in confidence; or
- **its readership** – such as for finance use only, private and confidential.

A key element of protective marking is that it involves a level of process: when a document is created or modified, for example, it will need to be assigned a classification, which then indicates how the document is to be treated.

A 'commercial in confidence' document, for example, might only be viewable by a third party if a non-disclosure agreement has been signed.[2]

For the purposes of the security architecture, if an information asset is marked as 'company confidential', then it needs to be treated as such. This does put more of a burden on the business to define which kinds of information are more of value and potentially at risk than others. Indeed, the ultimate authority of what is in scope has to be the business, as only lines of business can decide whether they care enough about specific information risks to do anything about them (and indeed, fund them).

Not only does the security architect lack the overall authority to decide these priorities, but also different parts of the organisation may have adopted different security practices in the past, or may have had different attitudes to risk – particularly if some departments were brought in through a merger, which is likely to be the case for larger companies. It is therefore up to senior business representatives – for example, through the aforementioned security architecture steering group – to be involved at this early stage to confirm where the thresholds lie.

Once this has been done, the security architect can propose the list of services and information assets considered to be in scope, the services they depend on and the physical locations they might occupy. In essence, it is the business-critical subset of all three that we want to consider, as shown in Figure 3.2.

A final area that needs to be taken into account is security management, audit and monitoring. Technology capabilities supporting these activities should always be considered within the scope of the security architecture.

---

[2] The UK government announced changes to its own protective marking scheme in April 2013, which came into force on 2 April 2014 (see Cabinet Office 2013).

Figure 3.2 Scoping should prioritise the business-critical subset of systems, services and information assets

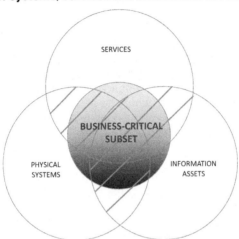

Case study example: the paint manufacturer's master discount list

As a case study example, consider the manufacturer with its list of discounts offered to major customers for its paint products. Following discussion, the business criticality of this information asset has become clear; less clear, however, is where it may be situated. While the 'master' discount list is stored in a controlled area of the corporate content management system (CMS), local copies also exist on the laptop computers of the finance director, sales director and head of marketing.

As the head of marketing does not have access to the area of the CMS in question, she has received a version by email – this information only came to light following an interview. This is not a problem in itself; however, the email system (where a copy of the list still resides) is not managed as securely as the CMS – for example, it can be accessed via both corporate-issue and personal smartphones and tablets.

Having assembled this information, the security architect then considers the places where the discount list is backed up or archived. Both the CMS and email system are backed up to the same system in the corporate data centre; however, the email server also offloads emails older than 60 days to an externally managed archive service. Corporate laptops are not backed up officially (they are not supposed to store corporate data), but it is common practice for individuals to back up their own laptops – indeed, the finance director backs up his laptop nightly to a USB stick, which he stores in a (usually locked, so he says) drawer at home. Finally, a copy of the CMS (and therefore the list) is held at a business continuity and disaster recovery (BC/DR) site, again managed by a third party.

As can be seen from the wide variety of places the master list (and other, equally sensitive files) might be stored, the security architect's job can very quickly become quite complex. At this early stage, it is best not to wade in with suggestions about how information might be better secured – astonished outbursts directed at board members might be counterproductive! However, situations such as this demonstrate how, with the best will in the world, some of an organisation's most critical information assets might not be very well secured at all.

THREAT AND VULNERABILITY ASSESSMENT

Once the scope of the security architecture has been defined (and, hopefully, confirmed by the steering group), the security architect can start mapping out the following:

- What risks exist to information and services, in what locations, based on both a solid understanding of the business and the **threats** it faces – these could involve threats caused by malice, stupidity, hardware failure or natural disaster, and could be internal or external.

- The technologies in use and the **vulnerabilities** they involve – these could be software bugs, configuration errors, weaknesses in management processes or user training, or indeed could be derived from poorly defined technology architecture.

Information about threats and vulnerabilities may already be available as part of existing risk assessments or registers, created, for example, as input to disaster recovery or business continuity planning. It can also come from:

- industry reports;
- technology press reports on recent attacks;
- vendor materials and security advisories;
- historical system and penetration tests;
- internal and independent security experts;
- audit and compliance assessment reports.

Identification of threats and vulnerabilities is not easy. According to a PwC survey released by the Department for Business Innovation and Skills (2013), over half of UK companies said they lacked resources to do this properly – though they did say they would have them in place sometime in 2014. The security architect should be able to know where to look, potentially recommending or using external experts (including **white hat hackers**) where appropriate. To reiterate the point, it is not the security architect's job to perform a thorough risk assessment of all business critical services and information assets. However, the security architect should be able to collate assessment results and recommend additional assessments should they not already exist.

Risk assessment can be **qualitative**, for example following a 1–5 scale for both probability and impact, as advocated by the UK government. Recalling that assets have potential vulnerabilities, in mathematical terms, we can compare relative risk in terms of probability times impact, the latter being measured in terms of cost to the organisation if it happens. As well as the impact of simple service failure and resulting loss of productivity, impact can be calculated based on the costs of:

- **Damage repair** – if information is lost, how expensive is it to replace it?
- **Brand reputation** – what might the cost be in terms of lost sales?
- **Root cause identification** – diagnosis can impose unexpected overheads and staffing bottlenecks.
- **Statutory failure** – the organisation may have to bear legal costs of breaking laws or regulations. Other measures can include revocation of licence to trade or restrictive penalties.
- **Post-audit** – some compliance laws require an audit trail of resolution steps following a breach.
- **Employment** – a breach may be a sackable offence, in which case a replacement will need to be found.

Assessment can also be **quantitative**, in which statistical maths and financial assessment methods are used to define the potential cost to an organisation. Quantitative risk analysis takes a more detailed view of the risk concerned – for example, estimating the actual costs should a person be prevented from working, or should a production line grind to a halt.

There are no hard-and-fast rules to risk assessment – it is up to the security architect to feel confident that existing assessments have delivered results in sufficient detail to enable the higher-priority risks to be identified and, therefore, treated. Some situations can be more complex than others – for example, an organisation providing temporary staffing services undertakes a salary payments run every month, the duration of which only lasts hours, but which needs to take place within a single day.

Note that the security architect is only concerned about risks to the organisation, its information assets and its continued ability to function. If an employee's personal device is stolen or hacked for example, and personal data is compromised, that is not of direct concern for the security architect.

Thinking once again about the question of scope, the security architect's assessment of threats and vulnerabilities should be sufficient to enable a security architecture design to take place. The output to the assessment stage will be documentation covering:

- Services and information assets that are in scope, together with their location in the IT architecture.

- Business criticality – so higher-risk, business-critical information assets and services can be treated as higher priority.

- The main threats and vulnerabilities faced by the organisation, and which information assets and services are affected by them.

- The compliance controls applicable to the business, and the business impact if they are not followed.

Where possible, these outputs should be presented and confirmed by a steering group before any further activities take place. Given that this group will have to sign off any subsequent recommendations, they should be expressed in a way that makes sense to business stakeholders – the simpler, the better.

ASSESSMENT OF EXISTING CONTROLS

Controls and processes play an important role in the security architecture, as a poorly configured or managed environment is also an insecure environment. Often it is the case that systems are well configured when they are first deployed, but over time, the configuration of a system fails to keep up with change, following a 'configuration decay curve'. Examples include where:

- usernames are still accessible even after someone has left the company;

- network ports or modem lines are left open when a system is no longer connected or used;

- integration points with other systems do not take into account new system features following upgrade.

To build a picture of existing controls and processes, the security architect needs access to materials describing how individual systems respond to certain events, in particular how services are provisioned to, and de-provisioned from, users, configuration management, patch management and so on – a more comprehensive list is provided in Chapter 4. This material can be made available from:

- IT policies such as the organisation's acceptable use policy (AUP) for corporate and personal equipment;

- HR and corporate procedures and practices, including clear desk policy;

- standard operating procedures for systems development, IT and network operations;

- working practices and existing business processes;

- training and awareness campaigns.

Existing working practices can also turn up security issues. For example, IT service development and delivery are rarely carried out exclusively in-house, resulting in a number of factors that need to be taken into account:

- The 'constant beta' process employed by some cloud service providers is inherently security-weak.

- Developers may work in an insecure environment, or may use an insecure cloud hosting service.

- Test data may be stored in an unsuitable jurisdiction, or in a way that breaks governance rules.

- The supplier could go out of business, be resource-deficient, or open to external attack.

In addition, all the security features in the world can be reduced to naught due to poor practice. Senior executives can nullify the best security controls by printing off confidential information and taking it home in a briefcase, for example. While the security architect's role does not encompass policing how well existing controls are enforced, he or she nonetheless needs to take into account how good the organisation is at sticking to the rules.

An understanding of controls and processes may lead to the identification of further vulnerabilities, which can then be taken into account in the next stage of activities – domain definition.

DOMAIN DEFINITION

Having collated, assessed and reviewed the current environment and required situation to an appropriate level, the security architect is now in a position to define something approaching a security architecture. As already mentioned, this involves adding a layer of security detail to the IT architecture within scope. Equally, it should be abundantly clear by this point that the security architect cannot possibly 'boil the ocean' and secure absolutely everything in sight, to mitigate every possible risk.

To respond to both of these points, the next activity is to define security domains – that is, well-bounded areas of the IT architecture with similar security requirements, which therefore require similar policies and controls. Not only this but once security domains have been defined, it should be easier to see which should be treated first – a major tool when it comes to responding to concerns about scope.

Security domains can be:

- **Physical** – for example, a domain could constitute the corporate data centre and everything within it, a certain set of computer servers and storage, or the public areas of a corporate headquarters.

- **Logical** – for example, a domain could consist of a certain set of systems or information assets that need to be protected, or different layers of the IT architecture.

- **Role-based** – for example, development domains used by system developers, or management domains used by operational staff.

- **Situational** – for example, an organisation may have a business continuity or disaster recovery domain, or may create a domain for data that needs to conform to compliance criteria (such as PCI-DSS).

Connectivity paths between domains can represent a domain of their own – for example, the 'de-militarised zone' (DMZ) refers to the technology environment that sits between the corporate network and the internet. The DMZ contains websites, routing gateways and so on, all of which (the security architect must assume) can be accessed by the general public.

Once security domains are created, they can be assigned **trust levels** ranging from 'wholly untrusted' domains, for example allowing public or guest access, to 'wholly trusted' domains, such as those containing core business systems and services, or which are subject to regulatory compliance criteria.

Relationships between security domains provide an indication of what security controls will be necessary. As shown in Figure 3.3, for example, if a less trusted domain requires access to a more trusted domain, some form of authentication will be required. Where an office desktop is connecting to a corporate system in an internal data centre, only one stage of authentication will need to exist; however, if a home laptop is required to connect to the same system, it will need to connect to the internet, then to a VPN before it can connect to the system concerned.

Figure 3.3 Security controls can be positioned at the edges of security domains

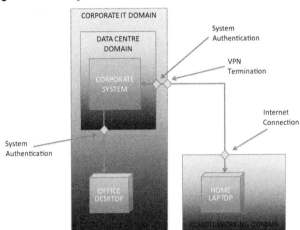

Definition of security domains follows guidelines similar to those for more general IT architecture good practice. The fact that systems should consist of modular subsystems, which perform their own function well without requiring too much from other subsystems, is an understood element of a well-designed architecture for example. In security terms, it is equally important to minimise the number of dependencies (coupling) between domains, as well as ensuring that each domain contains elements with largely the same security requirements (cohesion).

Architectural modularity also aligns closely with the concept of defence in depth. All too often, when things go wrong with computer systems, the underlying cause is not a problem in one subsystem or another, but in the way they interact. In the same way, security issues can manifest themselves in one (sub)system due to the weaknesses of another – for example, failure to authorise a person on one computer system, coupled with poorly configured shared credentials on another system, can result in a breach.

To enhance security, therefore, a crucial weapon in the security architect's arsenal is to understand the characteristics of well-designed, modular systems. The security architect should be able to spot areas where poor separation of systems exists, and to make recommendations to improve the systems or mitigate the risks that are caused. For example:

- Using a separate network for guest access, such as a separate Wi-Fi network, or ensuring that the computer in the reception area is not connected to the corporate LAN. This not only limits access to connected systems, but also minimises the risk of 'sniffing' data on the network. Also, using separate network paths such as virtual private networks and/or virtual LANs.

- Keeping tabs on virtual machine locations so that virtual machines (VMs) handling business-critical data are kept separate from those handling less sensitive data, which may have less restrictive security controls.

- Ensuring that applications and application interfaces are written to minimise coupling and maximise cohesion – as discussed above, these are tenets of good software design.

- Minimising the connections between live, development and training systems and services, and ensuring any data transfers between them are subject to stringent controls. This is stipulated in the ISO 27000 series of standards; it also reflects the Data Protection Act (DPA) in terms of how information is processed, whether information should be **anonymised** between systems, and so on. Simply put, developers may not be cleared to see real customer data or other confidential information.

In a worst-case scenario, the result of the security domain definition exercise may be a realisation that the architectures in use by the organisation, or those being proposed as part of a new IT solution, are potentially flawed. It is for the security architect to decide if recommended domain definitions are so important that failing to implement them will leave the organisation open to significant threat or regulatory sanction – to the extent that it needs to be flagged at board level.

At the end of this stage, the organisation should have a clear picture – indeed, it may well be a picture – of the security domains required, their trust levels and the relationships that need to exist between them, as well as appropriate regulatory compliance and audit criteria. These will need to be signed off by the steering group.

Case study example: the pharmaceutical firm looking to share research and clinical trials data

A pharmaceutical firm is looking to engage better with academic research institutions, in particular to share raw research and clinical trials data. Hitherto, the organisation has operated very much a 'closed' IT environment and as such has not needed to consider external access to its research data sources. One option would be to give academic institutions direct access to corporate systems or databases; however, this poses many questions in terms of both technical security and, for example, the vetting of academic staff.

Having decided that direct access creates too great a business risk, the organisation considers multiple possible options including the following. Each option suggests a different kind of security domain structure:

- **Option 1** – creating anonymised data sets based on data extracted from existing systems, checked and then delivered. This assures control over what is released but then makes it difficult to control what happens to the data, for example it could be copied and redistributed very easily. It also adds an administrative overhead (e.g. version control of data sets) while restricting flexibility.

  Retain existing domain structure, but with new technical and operational controls.

- **Option 2** – providing new database systems with the express purpose of managing anonymised data, which is extracted from existing systems and then loaded into the new systems. This solves some of the issues in Option 1, for example it becomes easier to restrict functionality. However, it then presents an overhead in terms of managing a potentially broad pool of users.

  Create new domain for external access, with controls on boundaries with existing domain and externally.

- **Option 3** – work with a separate 'gatekeeper' organisation that manages a number of cloud-based services on behalf of the company. Data is provided on a near-real-time basis to the external organisation which then creates facilities for academic institutions to analyse and interpret the data, as well as making certain 'open' data pools available for wider access.

  Corporate domain structure as Option 1; new organisation will require its own domain structure.

After some consideration, the firm decides to work with a partner to adopt Option 3. While this requires a new set of interfaces, it means that a third party is now responsible for managing academic relationships, provisioning access and so on, and enables a tighter set of controls to be created between the firm and the partner.

SPECIFICATION OF CONTROLS

The security design can be specified in terms of the **security controls** implemented at appropriate points in the security architecture – either within security domains to ensure the correct level of protection or at the interface between security domains to control access.

It is during this specification stage that the heavy lifting of the security architect takes place, as he or she proposes security mechanisms and identifies where they should be situated in the IT architecture. Security controls can be applied to the technical architecture in a number of ways, both within and across domains. As shown in Figure 3.4, the IT environment can be considered in terms of layers, each of which can be enhanced with different types of security controls:

- End-point **devices** can be desktop and laptop computers, mobile phones, tablets and an increasing variety of other devices. For example, a 'smart' thermostat or even a toaster may be a valid (and therefore 'hackable') device.

- The **network** extends across LAN and WAN, and also includes local networks in public and client locations, internet, wireless and mobile connectivity.

- **Servers** may be situated at office locations or data centres, in co-location facilities, or may be hosted in the cloud. These may be physical or virtual.

- **Applications** constitute databases, management and control solutions, enterprise and other software stacks, middleware and interface logic as well as front-end applications, which may be server, appliance, web or device-based.

Figure 3.4 The IT environment can also be considered in terms of layers

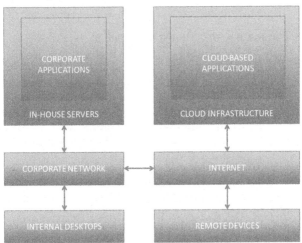

Having mapped out the IT environment in such a way, specifying the security architecture becomes a case of applying a security overlay to existing IT architectures, essentially to respond to the security needs of the following:

- where confidential data exists, at rest or in transit, and to what risks it might be subjected;

- where systems and end-points are located and what connectivity exists between them, in which locations and jurisdictions;

- as a result of the two points above: where data needs to be encrypted, to what level, and where it can exist 'in clear';

- where the edges or gateways exist that need to be protected, to be accessible by authenticated users and systems only;

- what other controls need to be situated at which points in order to reduce any other risks to information confidentiality, integrity and availability.

So which mechanisms will be most appropriate, given that multiple options may exist? As a starting point, the shortlist of security controls needs to have one of the following effects on the risk concerned:

- **Eliminate** – also known as 'avoid' or 'terminate', this includes preventative controls that remove the risk entirely, for example by replacing the equipment causing the risk, changing a working practice or relocating parts of the business to a more secure area. While elimination may not appear the easy option, it can sometimes be achieved by a level of lateral thinking. For example, it is worth confirming that a person or role needs to access a confidential information source in the first place, or whether a given system or computer service is entirely necessary. Elimination is particularly useful where it is commercially and operationally advantageous to move elements out of scope, for example to enable PCI-DSS compliance.

- **Reduce** – in the knowledge that it will not always be possible to remove a given risk altogether, this refers to limiting the probability of something going wrong by implementing security mechanisms, policies, or indeed both. Risk reduction or mitigation is the most common type of security control, augmenting the security in place by 'hardening' the service concerned or by ensuring that the policies and processes around its use are sufficiently robust. By nature, there will always remain a level of residual risk, which must fall below the organisation's risk appetite.

- **Transfer** – this is about sharing the burden of the risk with another party, for example by setting specific terms in the contract with a service provider or outsourcing company, or by insuring against the risk. It may be cheaper to insure against a loss than to try to prevent it. This is a question that can be answered through quantitative risk analysis. Risks can also be transferred by use of recovery mechanisms: for example, it may be cheaper to restore data from a backup than to implement onerous controls that prevent its accidental deletion. In this case, recovery time objectives – stipulations on the time taken to return information or service to a level that is deemed adequate – need to be taken into account.

- **Accept** – this refers to the recognition that the risk exists but that any actions to remove, reduce or transfer it would be too expensive. This can be the most practical response for lower-level risks whose mitigation could have a broad impact on the business. For example, use of unsecure apps together with corporate data on personal smartphones may be unadvisable, but options to deploy management software, to tell staff (including board members) not to do it, or to create unwieldy policies that would be ignored are unattractive. The only realistic approach may be for the security architect to explicitly say that a risk has been accepted (and, if possible, get board sign-off of the fact) rather than struggling to implement any alternative solution.

The result is a logical security architecture – that is, one which specifies security controls in principle, but does not provide any detail in terms of security vendors, product features and so on. The goal is not to boil the ocean, but to create a baseline – that is, a set of controls that acts within and between elements of the IT architecture to bring levels of risk to an acceptable level. Each area of the security architecture may have several candidate options.

For example, consider a 'standard' email service. In general, email information is sent 'in clear', that is, without being encrypted – this brings an inherent risk to confidentiality, for example should the email content be seen by someone other than its intended recipient. To reduce this risk, confidential information can be encrypted, either in terms of the entire email or an attached document; alternatively, the information can be kept 'in clear' as long as the network connection is encrypted, for example using a Secure Sockets Layer (SSL) connection to the email server or a VPN.

Given the plethora of potential options, the security architect should check the resulting logical security architecture for duplication and remove any redundancy, for example by consolidating access controls. The architect should also look for mechanisms that have the potential to undermine each other, or indeed, be counterproductive. For example, an overbearing authentication mechanism or one that requires a large amount of configuration (such as frequent password changes) may well result in system users choosing another, less secure mechanism for information exchange.

The resulting alternatives can each be presented as a number of 'architecture diagrams' that show each component of a given service, overlaid by security controls. The security architect should be able to consider each and assess their relative strengths and weaknesses in terms of their relative ability to mitigate risks, and recommend the more suitable alternative.

While there is no such thing as a 'standard' security architecture, guidance is emerging around security architecture patterns. The broader discipline of IT and software architecture patterns is over a decade old, being the standardisation of recognised solutions to recurring architectural problems – 'client–server' and 'thin-client' are commonly referenced examples. Security architecture can also benefit from a similar, patterns-based approach.

Organisations such as Open Security Architecture are making a number of architectural patterns freely available for general use. As shown in Figure 3.5, these include a Public Web Server

---

Figure 3.5 The Open Security Architecture pattern for a public web server

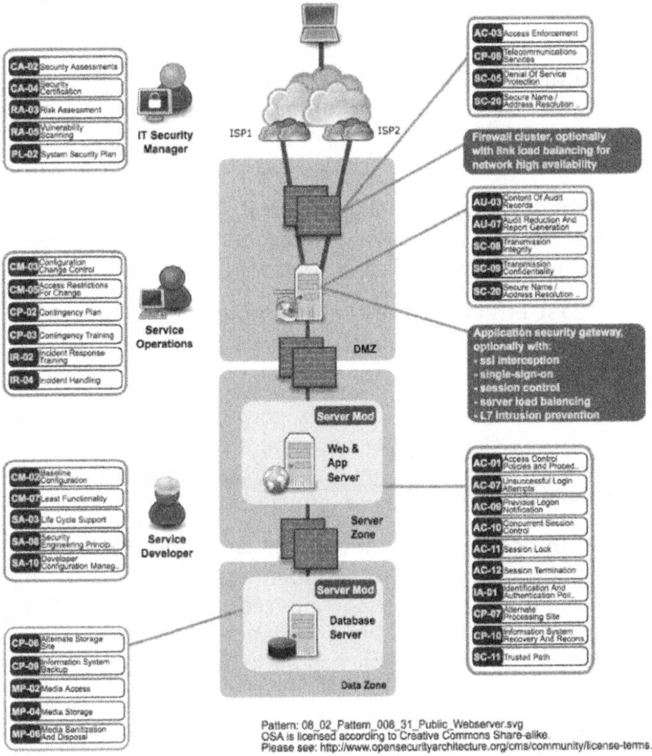

Pattern: 08_02_Pattern_008_31_Public_Webserver.svg
OSA is licensed according to Creative Commons Share-alike.
Please see: http://www.opensecurityarchitecture.org/cms/community/license-terms.

Pattern,[3] together with the controls required at each point. Note how the term 'zone' is used to mean security domain in this example – as noted in the introduction, the security world has yet to fully standardise its security architecture terminology.

EVALUATION OF OPTIONS

Once a logical security architecture has been developed, it can be translated into a physical security architecture, for example by applying real security products from specific vendors. As well as offering an appropriate response to the identified risks, security controls used as part of the security architecture should be equally appropriate in a technical sense. In particular, they should be:

- **Simple, scalable and manageable.** The controls need to be straightforward to both use and manage, and aligned with the working practices of the organisation, otherwise they may be worked around.

- **Vendor- and technology-neutral.** This may not always be possible, particularly if the organisation already has existing technologies or preferred suppliers in place.

- **Cost-effective.** The cost of implementing a control should be less than the estimated cost of something going wrong.

- **Fail-safe.** Having a single control can be a risk: a strongly locked door could be a problem if you lose the key, and if the key falls into the wrong hands, you may want to have another way of locking the door.

- **Conformant with standards and guidelines.** For example, a control should enable the level of monitoring and reporting required according to guidance such as the International Security Forum Standard of Good Practice for Information Assurance or PCI-DSS.

---

[3] http://www.opensecurityarchitecture.org/cms/library/patternlandscape/222-pattern-public-web-server

In addition to security controls, the security architect should be able to recommend mechanisms to monitor the security of the environment, report if failures occur and help diagnose and resolve any issues. In the context of information assurance, these mechanisms are referred to as 'protective monitoring', as documented by Good Practice Guide (GPG) 13.[4] Such mechanisms are often built into security controls, so for example an anti-malware package may report when a virus or a trojan has been identified.

Note that different products and services may have very different cost models – for example, a cloud-based email scanning service may work on the basis of a low cost per user per month, whereas a message scanning appliance could have a greater up-front cost but lower ongoing cost. Some vendors may bundle security products together, which individually offer a partial match to the need but which together are more than required.

Once options have been selected, they may require piloting and testing, for example evaluating solutions from multiple suppliers, which might take place before or after the business-case stage below. Further information on security testing – including testing of security controls – is given in Chapter 5.

The result of this and the previous stage can be delivered as a security architecture document, to be presented to the organisation (potentially via the steering group) for approval. It can exist as a stand-alone document or may become a chapter in the IT architecture document. In either case it should exist as a deliverable, such that it can be reviewed, updated and signed off. A potential structure is as follows:

- Services and information assets considered to be within scope – including definition of out-of-scope areas, for completeness.

---

[4] A commentary on GPG13 is available at http://www.freeformdynamics.com/fullarticle_subscribe.asp?aid=1087

- Threats, vulnerabilities and existing weaknesses that need to be treated, shown in existing architecture documents – the 'as-is' model.

- Proposed security domains and controls – mechanisms that can address vulnerabilities and reduce risks – the 'to-be' model.

- Ramifications and costs – in terms of capital outlay, operational costs, training and procedural impact – these will be picked up in the next stage (business case).

- Logging and alerting requirements – measures and events that need to be logged and stored to enable monitoring, diagnosis and resolution of faults.

- Management requirements – impact on existing structures, roles and responsibilities both internally and externally.

- Change controls – requirements on existing systems and controls to ensure that the security architecture is maintained at an acceptable level of risk, including reviews and audits.

- Audit and compliance requirements (including mandatory requirements).

A checklist for the security architecture document is given in the Appendix. Keep in mind, however, the high likelihood that some of the systems and services being secured will either be too complex or disparate for an 'ideal' security solution to be identified. The proposed recommendations or security mechanisms need to be appropriate to the identified degree of risk on the one hand, and workable and achievable on the other.

BUSINESS CASE

Assuming that it has been possible to design a practical, comprehensive security architecture, the next step is to present to technical and line-of-business directors the rationale for making a strategic investment in security controls that will enhance the enterprise or IT architecture and protect the business from the potential detrimental effects of a breach or non-compliance. In the simplest terms, the business case should provide a clear statement of costs of the preferred security architecture, together with its benefits to the organisation.

As well as the products and services involved, the business case needs to take into account non-technical security controls to be deployed – that is, procedures, policies and guidelines. These also come at a cost in terms of educating staff, gaining their buy-in for adoption and so on – for example, it may be necessary to conduct training seminars or pay for online help content. The security architect should be as transparent as possible about such 'hidden' aspects: avoiding mention of such things may come back and bite later if costs appear to rise unnecessarily.

How should the business case be presented to the organisation's senior management? According to security architect Tim Scammell (2003), the best approach is to deliver a presentation, for example offering a view of:

- the current state of the technical or enterprise architecture versus the future state of the architecture, that is, with security controls incorporated;

- a description of what is required in terms of the security controls and monitoring mechanisms, their ramifications and costs;

- benefits to be felt by the business, not only in terms of reduced risk but also potential opportunities for 'business enablement';

- a risk summary, based on the organisation's risk profile before and after the measures have been deployed;

- opportunities for 'quick wins' – that is, security controls that can be deployed at relatively low cost and with significant benefit;

- where a phased roll-out would be required, what each phase would involve, its prerequisites and outputs;

- finally, a comprehensive financial analysis of the costs, in terms of both up-front capital and ongoing operational expenditure.

The presentation should be kept succinct, expressed in clear, business-oriented terms. A picture is worth a thousand words – it is best to use diagrams representing the architecture and to show where security controls will be applied, rather than using long-winded text.

While the above list mentions 'business enablement', there is some debate over whether information security can have genuine, measurable business return on investment, beyond reducing risks. It can, if it enables the business to do things that were not possible previously, potentially because they were too high risk. For example, security controls may better support home working, improve sales-force productivity or enable a move into previously inaccessible geographies. Similarly, deployment of an application might be restricted due to security fears about end-point devices, or compliance certification may open up the opportunity to work with defence or government customers. Good security increases confidence and enables staff to act, while poor security can reduce the business's ability to deliver, as both confidence and trust levels are lower.

While the security architect should not overplay the 'business enablement' card, such examples demonstrate how the costs of the security architecture could be offset. Tangible examples of how information security helps the business are essential to gain the support of senior stakeholders, who might see it as no more than a cost. The security architect's role requires influencing such decision-makers to comply with architectural principles and objectives: if buy-in cannot be achieved at this senior level, it is less likely to carry much weight further down the chain of command.

IMPLEMENTATION

Assuming that the business case for security architecture is approved either directly or with modification, then implementation 'simply' becomes a case of procuring, deploying and configuring technical security controls, at the same time as deploying procedures, policies and guidelines. From this point, as indicated earlier, the security architecture might revert to being an element of a solution architecture, with controls to be rolled out alongside an ongoing systems deployment. Alternatively, where security controls are to be deployed across an existing enterprise or IT architecture, the security architecture can become a deployment project in its own right.

In either case and in much the same way as any other IT deployment, the steps involved in implementation are well documented, not least in terms of project management good practice which takes a project from planning, through procurement, to deployment and testing. At this stage the security architect becomes a consultant to the project, providing advice to technical and business staff to ensure that the security architecture is implemented successfully.

Describing the general principles of good project, programme and change management is outside the scope of this book.[5] However, specific facets of the security architect's role during implementation include the following:

- explaining information assurance and architectural problems to technical management and staff;

- securely configuring IT systems in compliance with their approved security architectures;

- testing the resulting environment to ensure it meets the specified security requirements;

- defining realistic policies, procedures and guidelines to ensure that the resulting architecture is not undermined by poor practice;

- establishing training programmes for security and IT professionals, to understand the security architecture and how it is mitigating risks;

---

5 BCS has a certification process for project management – for further information, see http://certifications.bcs.org/category/17903

- educating line-of-business management and staff in the policies, procedures and guidelines that make up part of the architecture;

- confirming that the implementation life cycle is followed according to good security practice, to ensure that it does not create new risks;

- mentoring, supervising and taking responsibility for the work of security professionals whose role will be to manage the controls being deployed.

The ultimate keepers of the keys of corporate security are the organisation's staff, whose actions can make or break a successful security architecture. A broader role for the security architect in this stage is outreach, helping ensure that security is viewed positively by all levels of the business rather than a bureaucratic drudge. A little advice can go a long way in making people more risk-aware, vigilant and prepared to follow security guidance around the security architecture, particularly when they understand how easily it could be undermined. For example, employees may not understand the dangers of:

- installing a wireless booster in the office to extend the network signal – poorly configured, it could open the corporate LAN to anybody else;

- allowing a family member to browse the internet via the corporate VPN, given that some websites may be (inadvertent or deliberate) hosts to spyware.

It is also useful to explain how certain regulations apply, for example the DPA or PCI-DSS and their impact on how personal information is processed, stored and protected. The security architect can and indeed should get involved with security awareness and education programmes where they exist, and recommend them where they do not.

MONITORING AND REVIEW

Given that new threats are emerging all the time, creating a security architecture should not be seen as a one-shot process. At the sharp end of security, for example, is the notion of the 'zero-day attack' – that is, a security issue that emerges out of the blue and could have a severe impact on corporate systems and/or risks if it is not dealt with quickly.

In particular, the organisation's risk-management process (there should be one) should be regularly looking for new threats, analysing them in terms of likelihood and impact, and keeping the security architect informed so that the security architecture can be updated if necessary, potentially to the extent of reiterating the stages we present here.

4 THE SECURITY ARCHITECT'S ROLE AND SKILL SET

As we have seen, the purpose of security architecture is to define the measures necessary to ensure that the IT environment appropriately protects the information assets and service delivery capabilities of the business, thus responding to the requirements set out in the IT security strategy. In principle, then, the security architect's job is to specify these measures and oversee their successful deployment.

A more formal definition, taken from the CESG definition for information assurance architects, is as follows:

[The security architect drives] beneficial security change into the business through the development or review of architectures so that they:

- fit business requirements for security;
- mitigate the risks and conform to the relevant security policies;
- balance information risk against cost of counter-measures.[1]

As should be amply clear by now, the security architect's job is unlikely to be straightforward. The complexity of the organisation within which he or she is working, the quickly changing problem space and the challenges of dealing with people at all levels mean this is not a job for the fainthearted.

---

[1] http://certifications.bcs.org/upload/pdf/cesg-certification-for-ia-specialists.pdf

From one perspective, the role could be seen as an efficiency-saving measure, taking on the challenge of addressing security architecture requirements so that other people in the organisation do not have to. While this is simplistic, it is important to note that the security architect acts as much as a facilitator as a doer. For example, system designers may see security aspects as lower priority than functional aspects of their designs. In response, security architecture needs a champion, someone who can treat its definition and deployment as a first priority.

In practice, there is nothing simple about making this happen. The security architect may face a wealth of conflicting requirements: of incomplete or inadequate policy documents; of an ever-changing regulatory and compliance landscape; of insufficient or non-existent senior buy-in. Against this quite onerous background, the security architect has a number of responsibilities:

- to act as liaison between the business and technology from a security perspective;
- to maintain an overview of the environment/landscape as a whole and its security aspects;
- to understand business strategy and how it relates to security strategy;
- to act as liaison between the appropriate regulatory bodies, IT auditors and the business;
- to educate IT and enterprise roles in the need for, and consequences of, reducing information-related risk;
- ultimately, to drive organisational change at all levels of the business.

The security architect's role is decidedly hands-on. He or she needs to be able to apply architectural principles to all kinds of security design, simple and complex, discrete and disparate. This becomes particularly important in the non-siloed, highly distributed world of technology and business we see today. The security architect needs to be able to understand practicalities when selecting security mechanisms from a number of perspectives, not least the sector they are in (for example, public sector use of G-Cloud), the scope of the IT environment and the specifics of the business context.

In this chapter we look at security, technical and business skills required by the security architect, but first, let us consider personal attributes. To achieve the successful delivery of security architecture, the security architect will also need to bring certain qualities to bear:

- **Speak and write in plain language.** The easier security architecture is to understand, the more likely it is to be implemented (and vice versa).

- **Be an expert in the art of the possible.** The security architect's role needs to be pragmatic, aligning with, or even enabling, other activities taking place across the business.

- **Focus on achievable goals.** Rather than trying to achieve all things for all people, the security architect should keep focused on the scope and goals that are set.

- **Know which battles to fight.** While some measures may be applied at a minimum, the absence of others could put the business in genuine jeopardy.

- **Keep market knowledge current.** The security architect needs to be aware of innovations in the security market, for example new offerings from vendors.

- **Catalyse policy, not policing.** The security architect should keep current on regulatory and compliance criteria, and use this knowledge to influence strategy.

- **Act as expert facilitator.** The security architect's role is frequently one of eliciting information from others, whether or not the answer is already believed to be known.

The security architect is, ultimately, a change maker. Neither the business nor IT departments will want to adopt security-related guidance without clear reason, so the security architect must also act as mentor and guide, however steep the climb. To design security controls that are achievable in practice, rather than simply some broad-brush statement of principles, it is up to the security architect to understand the organisation's attitudes, needs and constraints.

SECURITY SKILLS

While there have been volumes written about individual facets of information security practice (see the further reading section at the end of the book), in practical terms, the security architect should have a working knowledge of at least the following areas of security knowledge:

- prevalent types of threat;
- encryption and its role in information security;
- PCI-DSS and DPA criteria and operational principles;
- authentication and authorisation;
- identity management;
- technical and physical security controls;
- policies, procedures and guidelines.

We look into these below.

Prevalent types of threat

Since the dawn of computing, people have been looking for ways to break into computers, to access confidential information, or to deny access to others. Recent statistics do not make comfortable reading – a report for the Department for Business Innovation and Skills (2013) highlighted how the number of security incidents has increased since 2012, and indeed, is at 'an all-time high'. The median number of attacks on larger companies by an unauthorised outsider (including hacking attempts) had almost doubled since the same point a year ago, for example.

The constantly changing nature of the threat-landscape presents one of the biggest challenges for the security architect. Not only are the motivations of computer hackers increasingly complex (ranging from financial to political) and their attacks becoming more targeted, but no threat ever really goes away, even as new ones become prevalent. A number of 'traditional' threat types pervade, not least:

- **External intrusion** – building on attacks from traditional hackers, we are seeing an increase in 'brute force' attacks, which attempt to crack system and website passwords – the popular developer site Github was a 2013 casualty, for example.

- **Network snooping** – open Wi-Fi and pre-4G mobile networks are particularly susceptible to surveillance-based attacks, which can be tapped to watch for username/password combinations in unsecured traffic. Public hotspots and internet cafés are also common targets.

- **Malicious software** – viruses, trojans, worms and other forms of malware have been augmented and superseded by spyware, which can either log keystrokes on a local computer or act as part of a 'botnet' – a network of unsuspecting computers from which security attacks (such as distributed denial of service – see below) can be launched.

- **Insider breaches** – a significant proportion of attacks are instigated by internal sources. As well as the potential for unauthorised access, the so-called 'insider threat' can include fraud conducted by employees with a grudge. Threats can be greater if employees feel abused or mistreated – for example, in times of corporate restructuring or redundancy.

- **Data leakage** – this notion has emerged over recent years to describe security breaches ranging from industrial espionage and data theft to simple carelessness, such as emailing a confidential file to the wrong person.

- **Identity theft and fraud** – this involves use of one person's credentials to gain access to a system or service. Password theft may be done by external hackers, or staff may steal passwords from colleagues to access confidential information.

It can be difficult to identify and prevent new threats before they do any damage – as illustrated by the notion of the 'zero-day attack' mentioned in the previous chapter. In addition, white-hat hackers are uncovering new vulnerabilities and releasing their findings to the world without warning, creating a sometimes narrow window of opportunity for computer vendors to patch their software before hackers develop new exploits.

Building on such types of attack, we are also seeing 'attack vectors' that take more of an architectural approach to breaching confidentiality, integrity or availability. The range of attack vectors is broadening all the time, including:

- **(Distributed) denial of service (DDoS)** – an attack that prevents access to a service or information asset. DDoS attacks can use botnets to overwhelm websites with traffic, rendering them inaccessible.

- **Website hijacking** – new types of website attack are emerging all the time, including 'man-in-the-middle' attacks, which use a proxy to snoop on data as it passes through, or 'watering hole' attacks in which an innocuous website is infected with a spyware-downloading hack.

- **Targeted attacks** – these can combine technical vulnerabilities with social engineering – that is, psychological mechanisms designed to cause people to lower their guard. For example, 'phishing' emails can be used to get people to reveal passwords or other confidential information, which can then be used to hack into a computer system.

The security architect needs to have a good idea of the kinds of breach that are possible and/or likely, given the nature of the business, its organisation and working practices concerned. Some organisations – for example, in the defence, government, or oil and gas sectors – may be targeted by external attackers, as might research organisations or others reliant on their intellectual property – as illustrated by the 2007 incident of data theft in Formula One racing, involving a number of racing teams, including McLaren and Ferrari.

Many organisations have weak security processes, which will need to be tightened before it is worth putting in additional technical measures. Operational processes are a first port of call for improvement, particularly as many breaches relate to poorly configured or badly patched computer systems, leading to incidents that were completely preventable.

In addition, each kind of technology and deployment model can have its own security issues. For example, bespoke or commercial off-the-shelf software, installed in-house, will be open to different types of attack than outsourced software or cloud-based services accessed over the internet.

Encryption and its role in information security

Information security exists to protect information and services, both at rest and in motion. To this end, the fundamental enabling security feature used across security controls is **encryption** – that is, the encoding of information to protect its confidentiality and, to a lesser extent, integrity.

Cryptography – the science of encryption – has a long history in keeping information secure. The first documented reference of cryptography was in 700 BC, when the poet Archilochus referenced the 'scytale' – this involved wrapping a strip of leather around a stick, writing characters upon it, then unwrapping and filling the gaps with random characters (see Figure 4.1).

Figure 4.1 A scytale – one of the earliest forms of cryptography

Encryption methods in use today are based on using a key or cipher – that is, a string of characters used to encode information and render it unreadable based on a mathematical algorithm. Two options have emerged over the years:

- **Symmetric encryption,** which uses the same key to encrypt and decrypt the information. Also known as private key encryption (or indeed, secret key encryption, as it is important to keep the key secret), this method is used generally for data at rest, for example to encrypt specific files on a local server. It can also be used to encrypt information in transit, if the key can be transmitted to the recipient without compromising its confidentiality. Data Encryption Standard (DES), Triple-DES and Advanced Encryption Standard (AES) are all examples of symmetric encryption algorithms.

- **Asymmetric (public key) encryption,** which uses different encryption and decryption keys. This is used when information is to be transmitted to others, giving the recipient a 'public' encryption/decryption key to access the information. Examples include Rivest–Shamir–Adelman (RSA) and Digital Signature Standard (DSS).

Asymmetric encryption serves the purpose of 'non-repudiation' in that the recipient of an encrypted message can have reasonable confidence that:

- the sender of the message can be considered to be a trusted source;

- the message has not been changed in transit, assuring integrity.

Asymmetric encryption algorithms have a greater overhead than symmetric algorithms, which means that the former are often used to transmit a symmetric key, which is then used for a single communications session. This capability is built into the use of third-party certification authorities (CAs), which act as trusted third parties for hosting keys – a capability known as public key infrastructure. Given that the CA approach has come under frequent criticism due to a lack of diligence around the certificate issuing, one alternative is to use Pretty Good Privacy, which employs the concept of trust groups to share keys between trusted peers.

The security architect does not need a detailed grasp of the technicalities of encryption at an algorithmic level, apart from understanding its role in many of the security controls available today. As well as protecting against breach of confidentiality, encryption has a wide variety of uses across the security sphere:

- Encryption mechanisms can be built into email clients for both message encryption and transmission, though the former remains strangely underutilised.

- The SSL protocol uses encryption to create secure connections to websites – originally this was used for payment mechanisms, but it is also prevalent in social networking and email.

- VPNs use an encrypted communications 'tunnel' to protect the information from being snooped upon as it traverses the internet.

- Encryption also helps enable system and information availability, as encrypted data paths (such as VPN tunnels) make data sources harder to break into.

- Access control tokens, for example SecureID from RSA, enable generation of keys based on a time-stamp to support authentication and physical access mechanisms.

Note that use or export of strong encryption algorithms is often subject to country-specific laws or export criteria, such as the Wassenaar Arrangement,[2] which has been adopted by 41 countries to date. Such agreements can cause challenges for organisations that need to exchange confidential data with remote offices or suppliers in non-signatory countries.

Authentication and authorisation

Another, very important security feature is **authentication,** in which a person or system demonstrates their identity by way of a number of credentials, in general to gain access to a resource, such as a service or an information source. Authentication mechanisms can employ the following types of credential, in order of increasing security:

- **Something you know.** A password, PIN code or key question (to which only the person should know the answer). These are the least secure and the most open to social engineering attacks, in which a user is 'duped' into revealing the information concerned.

- **Something you have.** A token or tag that can generate a unique code (for example, the RSA SecureID token) or sending a code from a mobile phone application (app). While these are seen as more secure, a breach of RSA's own servers in 2011 showed that no protections should ever be taken as watertight.

---

[2] First ratified in 1996, the Wassenaar Arrangement on Export Controls for Conventional Arms and Dual-Use Goods and Technologies sets out a series of export controls on arms, telecommunications and computers, electronic equipment and information security algorithms, including encryption.

- **Something you are.** Biometric (fingerprint, iris scan) or other 'unique' information that can identify the physical person. These are seen as the most secure; particularly new forms of fingerprint reader that scan several layers of skin. However, even these mechanisms can be circumvented, for example by replicating the kinds of messages sent by the fingerprint reader to the server.

Authentication is single-factor if it uses just one of the above mechanisms, two-factor if it uses two, or multi-factor if it incorporates a greater number in the process. In general, access to simple services requires only single-factor authentication, but financial websites and a number of hosted corporate services (such as Gmail) now require two-factor authentication.

As well as enabling a trusted connection between people and technology, systems can authenticate to each other. For example, a computer can authenticate itself to a network entry point such as a Wi-Fi hub or a VPN server, or an email client can be preconfigured with user credentials to enable access to an email account.

Authentication needs to take place whenever there is a boundary to be crossed between security domains, and where trust levels are not already in alignment. So, for example, users may authenticate themselves to their own computer in a private user domain, which then has a trust relationship with the corporate IT domain, for example:

- A user may be able to log in to a corporate desktop using a username/password, and then access certain computer systems without needing to repeat the exercise (also called Single Sign On).

- A computer browser may hold user credentials for accessing one or more websites as 'cookies', again reducing the need to authenticate to individual sites.

- A management console may hold security credentials to enable remote access to the systems or services it manages.

- However, if a user is connected via a public domain, an additional level of authentication may be required to access the corporate domain – for example, it may be necessary to use a VPN.

It is important to note the relationship between authentication – which enables a person or system to say 'yes, it's me' – and authorisation/access control, in which computer systems and services allow specific access rights to individuals or other systems. Access rights can be expressed as:

- **discretionary access controls** such as read, write, execute access to files, folders/directories and programs, according to an access control list;

- **mandatory access controls,** used by more secure systems, provide more robust, policy-based access controls specific to individual services, files and users;

- **role-based access controls** assign users or systems to groups with predefined access rights;

- **digital rights management (DRM)** defines access controls within individual files, for example through built-in password protection.

As a general rule, access controls should be assigned according to the principle of least privilege – no single person should have blanket access to systems and services in the organisation. Least privilege can be difficult to enforce, however, particularly for deep-level administrative and technical roles. For example, a senior administrator working in a company for a few years in different systems administration roles can 'hoover up' access privileges as he or she changes from role to role. That individual could end up with the keys to the castle and as a result, the insider threat risk becomes significant.

User privileges can also be abused with spectacular results – consider recent cases of staff retaining access to the corporate Twitter feed even as they were laid off from a company, resulting in no little embarrassment to the company concerned! As a result, robust privilege review on role change or company departure should be integral to the processes involved, and strongly enforced. We return to the principles of provisioning and de-provisioning in the subsection on procedural security controls below.

Identity management

Authentication goes hand in hand with establishing **identity** – that is, the ability to link an identifier with a specific individual or a closely associated device. According to the BCS Reference Model for Professional Certificates in Enterprise and Solution Architecture, identity is defined as 'One or more data items (or attributes) that uniquely label an entity or actor instance'.

For example, identities can be applied to:

- people, using a passport number or username;
- computer systems, by processor identifier or using configuration information;
- mobile phones, which are uniquely identifiable via IMEI number;
- physical objects, using a radio frequency identifier (RFID) tag.

The goal of identity management is to enable an identity to be confirmed via a set of testable attributes. Identities do not have to be explicit – it may be sufficient for a public library to know that a person is demonstrably a student, for example upon presentation of a valid student ID, without needing to know any other details such as name or address. Equally, identities might only be loosely associated with an individual – for example, some anti-fraud technologies base their mechanisms on being able to identify a computer, device or web browser.

Given the inherent risks associated with identity (such as fraudulent access by stealing a username–password combination), authentication information needs to be created and managed securely. The standards body OASIS has created a model of identity management that uses Security Assertion Mark-up Language (SAML) and eXtensible Access Control Markup Language (XACML) to enable this information to be exchanged. The model incorporates the concept of a trusted third party – in the previous illustration, the public library could 'trust' the university to provide non-intrusive information about which people are valid students, for example.

Identity management is further complicated because roles and access requirements have a tendency to change frequently. In most larger organisations today, internal authentication and identity management approaches are based around a centrally managed directory, usually based on the Lightweight Directory Access Protocol ((LDAP) itself derived from the X.500 directory standard). Note also the availability of online identity stores, not least:

- OpenID offers a login (i.e. authentication) mechanism for specific websites.
- OAuth offers a broader range of authentication and authorisation services.

An increasing number of websites (including Facebook, Twitter, Google+ and associated services such as Klout) use an OAuth-based mechanism. What such sites do not say explicitly is that logging in to a website via a social network provider also gives the latter access to the user's activities while logged in to the former. This is seen by some security professionals as a social engineering-based privacy breach.

Technical security controls

As well as being an expert in potential types of attack, security strategy and IT architecture, the security architect is expected to be an expert across the range of available security controls. We have already discussed the notions of security domains and trust levels, enabling the architecture in scope to be divided into sections with shared security requirements.

A number of controls exist for protecting system elements from malicious access or other risks, both within and between domains. These include:

- **Secure communications protocols** – for example, SSL or Transport Layer Security can be used to secure Internet Protocol traffic.

- **Firewalls and VPNs** – minimising the potential for unauthorised access between trusted domains.

- **Data leakage prevention and protection** – scans outgoing content in emails and web-based transfers to ensure no confidential information is leaving the organisation.

- **Web access and content controls** – to restrict access to certain websites or to allow only certain content types.

- **Intrusion detection and prevention systems (IDS/ IPS)** – these analyse network logs to identify when an intrusion takes place and/or to block it from happening.

- **End-point protection** – including malware protection, personal firewall and access control tools to protect end-point devices such as desktops, laptops, smartphones and tablet computers and removable media.

- **Security incident event management** – event logging and diagnostic tools to enable breaches to be identified and resolved.

- **Authentication and identity management** – as discussed above, mechanisms such as Kerberos and OAuth.

- **Audit and review tools** – automated programs and scripts that can check for vulnerabilities in a given environment.

Security controls can be built into existing products and services (such as HTTPS or public key certificates in web browsers), can be run stand-alone on a device, computer, server or specialist appliance, or be accessed as a cloud-based service. In addition, sensitive data in motion can be protected using not only security controls such as SSL or VPN, but also 'standard' networking features such as network segmentation or access lists.

One of the architect's jobs is to decide which combination of controls will be most appropriate. As well as direct procurement costs, controls will require a level of management and configuration, the overhead of which must also to be taken into account. The architect will also need to keep on top of new developments. New capabilities are emerging all the time, which may supersede or undermine existing controls. For example, sensors using Bluetooth, Near Field Communication or RFID enable a desktop computer to 'sense' when its user is not in proximity and lock its screen accordingly.

The market for such products is also changing, so architects will have their work cut out keeping abreast of developments. Note that the marketing of security products is frequently predicated on making problems look as scary as possible, so the security architect needs to keep a clear head and make decisions based on genuine reduction of risk, rather than risking a knee-jerk reaction to the 'latest' threat type.

Finally, the security controls and their management will also need to be secured, particularly given that they may touch many parts of the existing environment. For example, cloud-based security services can be accessed from anywhere on the internet and may also be subjected to brute force attacks. Equally, note that security documentation indicates what controls are in place and, therefore, where vulnerabilities might exist. As such, security documents should be released to people only on a need-to-know basis and protectively marked accordingly.

Policies, procedures and guidelines

Security controls do not have to be technical. Risks can be mitigated by adjustments to the architecture itself through 'security by design', or by incorporating additional domains such as the DMZ and/or virtual LANs to create additional layers of separation. In addition, the organisation can protect sensitive information with appropriate use of policies, procedures and guidelines:

- **Policies** express the 'rules of the house' at a high level, for example to indicate who is responsible for what, or what is the organisation's overall security stance. As already mentioned, the organisation should have an overall security policy that explains its statutory obligations, its attitude to risk, its information security approach and the implications in terms of critical systems, services and information covered.

- **Procedures** offer more detailed sets of steps to describe how an activity should take place – for example, in terms of what happens when a person is recruited to or leaves an organisation, or the processes around protective marking. Procedures should be seen as risk reduction mechanisms – an organisation does not want to get overcome by bureaucracy, which increases risk if procedures are avoided as a result.

- **Guidelines** offer more general guidance about an area. For example, codes of practice to be adopted by system and service users, such as 'when working at home, it is advisable to keep work equipment in a locked cupboard when not in use'. In many cases, these can be set in agreement with, or even defined by staff members.

Policies, procedures and guidelines need to fit with the standards, laws and regulations to which an organisation needs to comply (as described in Chapter 5), and therefore need to be signed off by the relevant authority. This could be the chief information officer, chief information security officer, human resources department or a legal representative of the organisation.

The resulting documentation makes up part of the organisation's security 'personality' and may be all some employees see of security measures and controls. A set of policies on a staff noticeboard, an emailed piece of guidance, a recorded seminar can go a long way to giving employees a view on what they can or should do. Note that they need to be workable and enforceable at all levels of the organisation – there is no point at all in banning a certain type of device from corporate use, only for the chief executive to use her own, completely disregarding the guidance!

Physical security controls

While the IT security architecture does not concern itself directly with physical security, security measures for the latter (such as door key codes, security guards and the like) can have a significant bearing on the protection in place. As such, the security architect should be considering how potentially very simple physical mechanisms can reduce, transfer or even remove risks – for example:

- Moving a printer from the reception area of a company to a more secure area, rather than trying to create complex controls (potentially at great cost) to ensure nothing confidential is printed.

- Door entry biometrics or CCTV may be used as a mechanism to 'log' who accessed the data centre, at what time.

- Screen guards prevent others seeing what is on a laptop computer screen in a public place, such as public transport or a café.

Similarly, even the most robust of security mechanisms can be completely undermined by the smallest physical mishap – consider, for example, the true story, discovered by a security assessor, of a computer equipment room door being left open during the day, propped open by a fire extinguisher to prevent the room from getting too hot! In this case, the best possible solution to reduce the risk was to fix the air conditioning.

As with logical security domains, the physical environment can be considered in terms of zones, each of which is assigned a security level according to the information that is processed. Clearly life becomes easier if physical zones and security domains are aligned – for example, a data centre could be seen as both – though this will not always be possible in practice.

While physical security may be deemed to lie outside the jurisdiction of IT security, the security architect may request that certain physical protections are implemented – such as key codes on doors. The alternative is to ensure that only data that is of an appropriate classification is processed within a certain physical space. It may also be necessary to consider how data moves through the building (for example, transport of tapes to enable off-site backups), locations of printers and so on. Of course, physical protections such as fire escapes, and the risks they mitigate, may need to take priority over information security requirements.

Also, while remote door locks, fingerprint scanners, anti-theft device locks, CCTV and so on may be considered as physical security mechanisms and the responsibility of building or facilities management, their technical components may need to be considered as elements of the security architecture, not least because all such devices generate information, which also needs to be handled securely.

It is becoming increasingly hard to see physical measures as anything other than valid elements of the security architecture – a situation which will be exacerbated by the Internet of Things, which will increasingly require the security of physical objects to be taken into consideration – for example, a hacker could disable the heating system and render a building unusable. 'Smart' appliances (including white goods) may also need to be considered as within the scope of the security architecture, if they bring new risks with them.

Physical security is covered in more detail in the BCS enterprise and solution reference model section 'Design for business security'.[3]

TECHNICAL SKILLS

Here we consider skills outside the security remit, including a working knowledge of:

- enterprise and IT architecture diagrams and models;
- technology development and procurement;
- systems and service management;
- backup/recovery, business continuity and disaster recovery;
- virtualisation and cloud computing.

Enterprise and IT architecture diagrams and models

To be able to have a constructive dialogue with those developing IT architectures, the security architect needs to be able to speak the same language as the group of people creating them. A number of enterprise architecture frameworks exist, including:

- **TOGAF** – originally based on the US DoD Technical Architecture Framework for Information Management, and now at Version 9, this is the most commonly cited enterprise architecture framework.

- **The Zachmann framework for enterprise architecture** – this encompasses several types of diagram to cover the what, how, where, who, when and why of the business and the systems that support it. Zachmann's models provide a good starting point for documenting the organisation, its processes and data flows.

---

[3] http://www.bcs.org/upload/pdf/reference-model-enterprise-solution-architecture.pdf

- **The Integrated Computer-Aided Manufacturing (ICAM) DEFinition (IDEF)** – a number of IDEF standards exist for modelling different kinds of system and process model, which may still be in common use.

Also of note is the Unified Modelling Language (UML), which can be used to capture information about business information requirements, processes and activities as well as system requirements, design and deployment features.

Within these frameworks, models exist for all elements of the security architecture, including logical and physical representations of systems, domains and trust levels, security information and events. With such a broad range of models available, it is not for the security architect to become an expert in all of them – particularly as many organisations choose to 'cherry-pick' elements of each. However, he or she should be able to interpret the diagrams produced by the organisation's system architects, in whatever form they take; to have a dialogue about them with the experts who created them; to modify them to incorporate security features for review; and finally, to incorporate feedback.

Technology development, procurement and deployment

IT risks can be inherent to the development, procurement and deployment process. For example, in the 'constant beta' model for software development, new versions of software are released to users before they might be considered fully functional – this model may not be the most beneficial in security terms, if security is considered as an afterthought. Similarly, data migration during an upgrade may expose the data to considerable risk if it is not handled in the right way. Security architects need to keep their wits about them to decide when it is necessary to tell the business to hold a release if it increases business risk to an unacceptable level.

In these areas, the role of the security architect is mostly a case of providing counsel. Taking development first, the security architect can educate organisations on how good security practice applies to in-house development activities, with a resulting influence on:

- **The requirements specification.** Security and security management features should be specified as system requirements, including those that enable interaction with the rest of the security architecture (for example, authentication).

- **The development cycle.** Security starts with the requirements specification for a new system or service, and ends with security tests being part of final acceptance testing. We shall look at security testing in Chapter 5.

- **The development environment.** The development environment needs to be conceived and constructed with security in mind, taking into account potential risks from accessing non-sanitised customer data, to the possibility of unvetted developers inserting back doors into the code.

- **Software source code.** Source code is an information asset in its own right, and needs to be protected accordingly. Security considerations include source code escrow, where code is kept with a third party in case something happens to the supplier, together with the conditions of its release.

- **Debug and event logs.** Information logs could contain confidential information and may need to be used as evidence in a court of law, and should be designed and protected appropriately.

Certain elements of the IT architecture are just as likely to be bought as built. As well as ensuring that the security of products and services is being procured, it is important to conduct supplier due diligence, in security terms – for example, ensuring that the supplier has implemented adequate measures to:

- protect against denial of service (DoS) attacks;
- ensure secure transfer of the data away from the supplier for whatever reason;
- enable data escrow in the event of the supplier going out of business;
- ensure that the supplier can evidence appropriate regulatory and compliance conditions.

Finally, the architect needs to understand the linkage between IT and business processes – that is, how and why humans and computers interact – and their security implications. Adding security 'features' to a design may simply be a case of ensuring that the right information is made accessible to the right people, at the right time – for example, a breach of confidentiality could be averted by preventing certain information from being displayed in the first place. Building on the principle of least privilege, a perfectly valid question is: 'Do you need that information at all?' If certain information is unnecessary, it may be better to remove it than have to deal with the (higher-risk, expensive) consequences. Indeed, both the DPA and PCI-DSS mandate such an approach.

Systems and service management

Systems management controls can also make or break a security architecture. Like any facility, computer systems and services degenerate over time; as they do so, the risks associated with them increase – for example, as old versions of software or configuration data become out of date. A well-managed system is by definition a more secure system.

A number of management controls exist, taken from frameworks and good practice approaches such as ITIL and COBIT, which can help assure the protection levels of individual systems, and therefore the security architecture as a whole. These include:

- **Asset management** – a major tool against attack is simply knowing what systems, desktops and other devices are connected to the network at any moment in time. In this current climate of BYOD, asset management principles need to be reinforced with acceptable use policies (see Chapter 5).

- **Patch management** – keeping a system or desktop updated with the latest software and security patches minimises the potential for attack. A poorly patched system will be more susceptible to zero-day attacks, for which patches should be installed as soon as they have been verified as fit for purpose.

- **Provisioning and de-provisioning** of devices, system and service access for users as they join the company, move departments, work on specific projects and leave the organisation. This is not always straightforward – for example, people sometimes want to take a phone number with them when they leave an organisation, and LinkedIn account details have been subject to legal dispute.

- **Configuration management** – that is, deciding in advance how a system should be configured and indeed 'hardened', which becomes even more important in the age of the virtual machine. Just using a standard-issue operating system or software download as the basis for a VM inevitably increases risk.

- **Desktop management and configuration** – including standard policies and security settings for office applications and web browsers. Locked-down desktops are simpler to manage and secure.

- **Access management.** Security architecture has a role both inside and outside systems. Each system should have appropriate access controls in place to ensure that only the right people can access the right information, on a 'need to know' basis. Ownership can be applied to designated people. PCI-DSS mandates that access to all in-scope PCI-DSS subject data environments is monitored and logged. This has to be evidenced on annual assessment and by IT audit.

- **Log management and system audits** – maintenance of system management records can be of significant benefit when diagnosing and resolving security breaches. It stands to reason that log data needs to be afforded quite a high level of protection, since if this is deleted, it will be more difficult to identify the cause of a breach. Retention of logs should be subject to the retention policy in force.

- **Staff vetting and access management** – unscrupulous admin staff may breach security, which brings us back to the idea of least privilege.

- **Change management.** Even the smallest changes in the business or technology can have a significant impact on the stability or integrity of the security architecture. Influential events can involve: external factors, such as legislation, new and emerging threats; new technology or change of use (for example, addition of a module); internal, such as changes in organisational structure, relocations of staff or departments; and fault-related, such as security breaches as well as fire, flood or theft. While change control mechanisms might be increasingly hard to enact for end-point devices given the expanding variety of devices and BYOD, core, business-critical systems should be subject to appropriate controls. IT security and data protection should be seen as integral to change assessment and approval policies and procedures.

The security architect should not only be able to incorporate these principles in architectural design thinking, but also be aware what risks are caused, or compliance breaches occur, if any of the above are absent or only weakly applied. For example, PCI-DSS mandates that IT systems and software considered to be in scope for PCI-DSS are kept up to date in respect of security patching and operating versions. The term 'baseline controls' refers to the minimum necessary that should be applied.

In the enterprise context, information security can be supported by the use of an information security management system (ISMS), which acts as the central source of information and oversight pertaining to the organisation's security. The ISMS may be supported by additional systems, products and services whose job it is to help security managers in their daily jobs.

The ISMS constitutes a fundamental element of the IT environment from a security perspective, not least because many ISMS systems now include compliance-specific elements such as PCI-DSS features. It makes sense, therefore, to consider the capabilities and needs of the ISMS when designing architectural controls, and to ensure that the ISMS is updated with any architecture decisions.

Backup/recovery, business continuity and disaster recovery (BC/DR)

As well as preserving the confidentiality of sensitive information, we are looking to protect its integrity and availability. These go hand in hand, in that good security is not only about prevention, but also about recovery should something go wrong. Examples are:

- provision of a fallback system with appropriate failover to mitigate against a DDoS attack;

- regular backing up of data in case of corruption or destruction.

While this is not the place to go into detail about the finer points of system resilience or backup strategy, it is worth mentioning the role of separation-of-concerns in backup and recovery. Keeping backups separate from online systems ensures that any security breach does not extend to the backup set, for example.

The bigger picture of integrity and availability leads to BC/DR, that is, ensuring that the organisation can continue to work in case of fire or flood, major security incident or other crisis situation. Good BC/DR practice follows a similar life cycle to security architecture, in that it involves risk assessment, definition and procurement of an appropriate response. BC/DR may be mandated in environments subject to compliance certification, such as PCI-DSS.

Where failover sites or equipment exist, the security architect should ensure that they are addressed as part of the overall security architecture. This includes treating the BC/DR plan – while its primary purpose is to enable the business to keep working, its deployment should not compromise the organisation's corporate or enterprise security policy (which would be ultimately counterproductive).

As well as user data, it is crucial to protect the integrity and availability of configuration data. This exists across the entire environment, but is not always managed very well – a fact that sometimes only becomes clear in crisis situations, for example as the organisation attempts to recreate a given service using mechanisms available from the BC/DR site. In other words, it is important to keep recoverable backups not only of user-generated data, but also of the information created and modified as systems and services are configured, provisioned and used.

Virtualisation and cloud computing

Virtualisation and cloud computing are having a major influence on IT architecture in general, and security architecture in particular. While they are treated as separate market trends, virtualisation is at the heart of dynamic IT architectures that underpin cloud computing, so it makes sense to consider them together from the perspective of technical skills requirements.

Indeed, while the term 'cloud computing' originally referred to externally hosted services, cloud-based models are just as likely to occur in enterprise data centres, particularly in information-rich, highly regulated industries such as banking. The Cloud Security Alliance (2011) defines four models for cloud computing, against which both data and services can be mapped:

- **public,** referring to hosted service delivery;
- **private,** internal/on-premise or external (including dedicated or shared infrastructure);
- **community,** shared between a closed group of members;
- **hybrid,** combining any/all of the above.

Cloud models can also be considered in terms of the services they provide, for example:

- **infrastructure as a service (IaaS)** – using pooled, virtualised resources for processing or storage;
- **platform as a service (PaaS)** – an application software stack is accessed from a provider;
- **software as a service (SaaS)** – entire applications are accessed via a web-based interface.

By understanding the proposed benefits of cloud-based models, we also gain an insight into potential security risks. At the heart of the cloud computing proposition are the gains to be had from shared use of highly managed, dynamically allocated resources. In principle, these enable greatly enhanced scalability (or 'elasticity') compared with a traditional system architecture. In addition, data and services are not locked to a specific server device and can be accessed from anywhere on the web.

This high degree of flexibility comes at a potential security cost. As well as the better-known risks around third-party hosting of services, we can see a number of new types of risk emerge, for example:

- **Runaway costs** – if hosted cloud resources are used to a great extent, the costs can become prohibitive.

It is possible that a hacker could cause additional processing and therefore expense.

- **Poor due diligence** – cloud service providers are hotbeds for start-ups, not all of which have security front-of-mind (but which may be adopted by business users without consulting a security expert).

- **Virtual machine sprawl** – because it is so easy to create new VMs, the numbers created can cause a management overhead and weaken the ability to secure the environment as a whole.

- **Console risk** – VMs and cloud services are usually managed through a central console, which itself needs to be secured or become the weakest link in the environment.

- **Dynamic movement risks** – cloud and virtualisation make it possible to relocate processing of confidential information to an untrusted zone (on- or off-site), with possible downstream DPA issues.

- **Location sensitivity** – cloud providers may move data through untrusted jurisdictions, or may be unable to reference exactly where that data is stored, which could break governance rules or national law.

- **Resilience risk** – cloud-based data management models (such as NoSQL databases) are faster than but not as resilient as traditional database management systems.

- **Information ownership** – the terms and conditions of some cloud providers (notably many social networking sites) attempt to claim ownership over content stored on their servers.

- **Destruction (lack of) guarantee** – it becomes difficult to ensure and evidence data deletion by service providers, either to meet compliance criteria or litigation, or should a contract be terminated.

- **Staff vetting and confidentiality** – while service providers may state that they will not access the confidential data, this may not offer sufficient guarantee without evidence of vetting procedures and, potentially, signing of client non-disclosure agreements.

To enhance the secure design of virtualisation and cloud-based services, a good starting point is (once again) to think first in terms of physical security zones – i.e. grouping which parts of which services are running in-house and which are hosted/outsourced. Once this has been done, and even if certain parts of the physical architecture lie outside corporate control, the security architect can consider how to ensure the security of the logical architecture in its entirety, regardless of who is doing the hosting.

While guidance is still developing in this area, two groups in particular are useful sources of information – The Open Group and the Cloud Security Alliance (CSA). The Open Group provides a checklist of criteria to be met by organisations looking to secure cloud services, as follows:

- **Weakest link** – suggesting the creation of a mediation layer to control access to cloud services, rather than allowing them to be accessed individually.

- **Off-line backup** – that a cloud service should allow for the extraction and backup of data to 'another environment of their choice'.

- **Policy-based service access** – linking to weakest link, to enable access by policy.

- **Data protection** – to enable compliance with regulatory standards, even given cloud principles such as multi-tenancy.

- **Privacy** – cloud services need to protect private information in the same way as any other corporate system.

- **Multi-tenancy** – the cloud solution needs to be able to protect individual client data and assets even if the underlying hardware is shared.

- **Data evacuation** – it should be possible to purge a cloud service of client data, for example on termination of that service.

- **Intellectual property** – cloud service providers and their associated supply chain need to respect the privacy and intellectual property requirements of their clients.

- **Accountability** – cloud providers should be able to provide monitoring and logging information as required for business and regulatory audits.

Meanwhile, the CSA has defined a set of principles that cloud service providers need to meet, 'to guide cloud vendors and to assist prospective cloud customers in assessing the overall security risk of a cloud provider' (CSA 2013). Now in its third edition, the Cloud Controls Matrix reads like a microcosm of good security architecture practice, covering:

- the availability of security standards (such as the Open Web Application Security Project for web applications) and open application programming interfaces to enable interoperability;

- auditability, including by independent bodies, and demonstrability of BCP and DR practice;

- asset, change and configuration management processes, including testing and in terms of both physical and virtualised assets;

- the ability to classify and label data according to applicable criteria;

- protection against fraudulent activity, notably around e-commerce;

- criteria around confidentiality including use by providers for self-testing and secure disposal;

- physical and technical security measures to protect hosting centres;

- identity, key and entitlement (authorisation) management mechanisms, including strong encryption and life-cycle management;

- governance, risk and compliance and HR principles and practices covering how the cloud service and information are managed and staffed;

- security incident management, diagnosis and resolution policies and procedures.

While virtualisation and cloud computing do appear to add complexity and undermine traditional security models, they also bring security benefits. For example, virtualisation offers increased resilience through VM snapshots, compartmentalisation and, indeed, separation of concerns – if a VM is compromised, others are protected.

Equally, hosted IT service providers and co-location facilities have the potential to be more secure and better at BC/DR than the organisation's own IT data centres. This makes sense – such providers should be just as stringent as in-house IT, if not more so given the multi-tenanted nature of the services they provide. As a result they can often do a better job, particularly around:

- **physical security** – hosting centres can offer high levels of physical protection;

- **business continuity** – many hosting providers operate out of multiple data centres;

- **resilience** – for example, Amazon Web Services security-tests all VMs against predefined security criteria before they can run.

However, while resilience does potentially become easier with the use of cloud-based systems, this should not simply be assumed by the security architect, who can provide guidance as cloud services are being procured. For example, will a provider offer access from time to time, to support a mandated programme of regular compliance audit and certification? Will the organisation be able to gain quick access to cloud-based services in case of a breach in a timely manner, according to formally agreed contract conditions? Such factors should not be taken as a given, of course – due diligence is essential.

Virtualisation and cloud computing are still maturing – for example, the ability to run encrypted VMs in the cloud is a relatively recent phenomenon – so security architects need to keep a watchful eye on developments and associated compliance regulation, and adjust both their thinking and their guidance, accordingly.

BUSINESS SKILLS

Given that security architects need to be able to have a constructive dialogue with the business, they require an understanding of a number of business concepts and their potential impact on the security architecture:

Statutory and industry frameworks. Different laws, regulations and governance requirements may apply, depending on the organisation's industry sector and the markets within which it operates. We have already mentioned the DPA and PCI-DSS, but security criteria can derive from a multitude of other sources – for example, guidelines from the UK Financial Conduct Authority require segregation of duties between computer systems, to prevent collusion. As regulatory principles are changing all the time, many organisations have legal teams to keep on top of the relationships between national, European and international law, standards certifications and other frameworks.

Equally, governance constraints can come from business contracts with suppliers and customers – for example, external organisations can impose criteria around management of personal data. Even quite innocuous-sounding schemes can have knock-on effects – for example, signing up to a 'green charter' could require environmental data to be stored and reported, and therefore secured.

Indeed, a company may choose to do business in certain countries or jurisdictions in order to benefit from their legal structures, or to enable access to local markets, which will bring their own security constraints. For example, a business may choose to be headquartered 'offshore', as is the case for Amazon's European operations. Not only do individual country criteria apply, but the security architect will also need to understand the legal and security ramifications of moving data from one jurisdiction to another.

Employment law. This can have an impact, for example in terms of how staff should be disciplined following what kind of breach, the notions of confidentiality and customer privacy, and duty of care to the organisation and other staff. An AUP may be attached to the contract of employment as an annex, to cover company assets and corporate data, breach of confidentiality, lack of personal protection against theft and also topics such as data theft and cyber-bullying.

Similar topics may need to be referenced in supplier and subcontractor contracts, which may be described as a security aspects letter as an appendix to the contract. These aspects should be treated as part of supplier due diligence during the initial procurement process, and indeed used as a checklist with existing suppliers.

Business attitude to risk. The business has an attitude to risk that is inherent in its business model. Some businesses will operate high-risk operations and may even sail close to the wind when it comes to business risk. Consider, for example, the 'fail-fast' business model: in this case the business is encouraged to try new working practices and learn from them if they do not work. For PCI-DSS, it is not unknown for businesses to make a conscious decision to accept short-term risk and pay fines resulting from breaches, to give them time to achieve compliant, auditable infrastructure and practices in the future.

Staff trust. Businesses can also vary the amount of trust they ascribe to both internal and external staff. For example, some organisations may have a tightly controlled, external 'guest' network, whereas others may allow subcontractors to connect to the corporate Wi-Fi. Again it is up to the security architecture to weigh up these considerations and provide guidance to the business and to IT about just how much risk is being created, such that the latter groups can decide whether it is acceptable or conformant with the organisation's defined or industry-related governance criteria.

Mergers and acquisitions. A merger will require bringing together several different system architectures and software environments. This could increase risk in a number of ways – for example, it may be necessary to integrate multiple software systems; or users may have to use unfamiliar systems; or it may be necessary to access systems remotely (from a new site) where previously they were only accessed locally. Policies set for one company may not fit with the systems of the other. As already mentioned, security architecture assessment may need to take into account the different security attitudes and polices of different parts of the company, and make decisions between them.

Demergers. A demerger will require the separation of systems, and therefore has a potential governance and security architecture impact. Equally, there could be disgruntled employees who consider damaging the systems of the other company, or attempting to access confidential information of the other company.

Outsourcing and offshoring. Perhaps counterintuitively, outsourcing can be more secure because it can require more stringent recruitment. However, it can also lead to increased risk. Consider the salutary example of offshoring in which local staff were bribed to release data. By nature, outsourcing requires reduced central control potentially increasing risk.

Just as the business environment is constantly changing, security should not be treated as a one-shot operation. It is up to the security architect to keep engaged and informed as the business moves forward, in a process of continuous evolution and, hopefully, improvement.

5 STANDARDS, TOOLS AND TECHNIQUES

Having looked at the security architect's skill set, in this section we consider what resources and tools are available for the role. First we look at an overview of available standards, guidance and advice. We then drill into guidance covering activities of security testing and operations.

STANDARDS, GUIDELINES AND REGULATIONS

Security standards tend to be set by national bodies such as the British Standards Institute in the UK, AFNOR in France or ANSI in the USA, or by international bodies such as the International Organization for Standardization (ISO). Many security standards already exist (and have been in place for decades), but given how quickly security architecture is developing as a discipline, it follows that standards are still relatively new. Where standards are in place, they are comprehensive but they tend to focus on individual systems and the processes and procedures required to manage them, rather than the IT environment as a whole.

Security architects require a working knowledge of these standards and should be able to apply the principles they espouse, as they set the scene and provide an overview of the techniques required for good security practice. Indeed, any security mechanisms proposed will have to conform to standards and certifications in place. However, they do not have to know the details – which generally do not offer specific guidance (if standards were too detailed, they would quickly go out of date).

Standards include the following:[1]

ISO/IEC 27001:2013 Information technology – Security techniques – Information security management systems – Requirements. This sets out the elements required in any security management system in terms of a process that runs from risk assessment through definition of controls, to definition of a management process. For the security architect, above all it offers the baseline upon which security architecture can be built.

ISO/IEC 27002:2013 Information technology – Security techniques – Code of practice for information security management.[2] The standard upon which information assurance is founded, this provides an expanded reference for the creation, implementation or maintenance of information security management systems. It offers general guidance on what constitutes an information security policy, access management, operational security and incident management as well as information covering such areas as human resource and physical security. It outlines a process for risk assessment (more detail is provided in ISO/IEC 27005) but tries not to be prescriptive in terms of controls.

ISO/IEC 27004:2009 Information technology – Security techniques – Information security management – Measurement. This provides guidance on measurement techniques and example measures.

ISO/IEC 27005 Information technology – Security techniques – Information security risk management. This offers a detailed, yet non-prescriptive process for risk assessment, analysis and mitigation. While this may not be the security architect's job, he or she should be able to work with the people responsible.

---

[1] The date attached to ISO standards indicates their last revision.

[2] The previous name for this ISO standard was ISO/IEC 17799:2005; it was based on the British standard BS7799.

ISO/IEC 24762:2008 Information technology – Security techniques – Guidelines for information and communications technology disaster recovery services. This offers guidance to business continuity planning, including a broader perspective of business and operational risks. For architects, it also provides guidance on capabilities and practices service providers should offer to ensure disaster recovery, which is increasingly relevant given cloud computing.

ISO/IEC 13335 – Guidelines for the management of IT security. We took our definitions from this earlier, which covers concepts, models, controls and techniques for IT security and its management. It is gradually being incorporated into other ISO standards.

ISO 15408 – The common criteria for information technology security evaluation. This rolls together other evaluation criteria, including information technology security evaluation criteria (ITSEC), to enable functional and acceptance testing with regard to security. It incorporates seven levels of rigour, from EAL1 to EAL7. EAL4 is generally seen as appropriate for most scenarios; above EAL5 tends to be for higher-security environments and specialist systems such as those used in government and security circles. Note also that EAL4 certificates are recognised by countries participating in the Common Criteria Recognition Arrangement.

One issue with existing standards is that they do not fully cover more leading-edge technology areas, such as:

- management of dynamic provision of resources, including VMs;
- acceptable use of personal equipment such as mobile phones and tablets;
- due diligence with respect to online services including hosted storage and communications.

In such fast-moving areas as these, traditional security guidance can be perceived as too onerous, which risks them being ignored. For example, provisioning of a traditional server may take a period of weeks, whereas a VM can be provisioned in a matter of seconds. In the latter case, even a half-hour set of security procedures may be perceived as too great an overhead.

Guidance for the fast-moving areas is emerging from a number of directions, including industry-driven initiatives and consortia, which have published standards and guidelines on:

Open Enterprise Security Architecture (2011). Published by The Open Group, this offers guidance on key concepts and principles behind enterprise security architectures, together with some guidance on how to implement one.[3]

Framework for Secure Collaboration-Oriented Architectures (2012). Also from The Open Group, this provides an overview of guidance on securing environments which do not depend on 'securing the corporate perimeter' – that is, most corporate environments today.[4] This work was originally undertaken by the Jericho Forum (also part of The Open Group).

Sherwood Applied Business Security Architecture – a free-to-use set of guidelines on security architecture. This defines five levels of security architecture – component, physical, logical, conceptual and contextual – in a similar way to the Zachmann framework, so may be familiar to enterprise architects who know the latter.[5] This has now been integrated into TOGAF.[6]

International Security Forum Standard of Good Practice for Information Assurance – this takes a business process view of security and offers guidance on how to deploy controls to protect business processes.

---

[3] https://www2.opengroup.org/ogsys/jsp/publications/PublicationDetails.jsp?publicationid=12380

[4] https://www2.opengroup.org/ogsys/jsp/publications/PublicationDetails.jsp?publicationid=12541

[5] http://www.sabsa-institute.com/members/sites/default/inline-files/SABSA_White_Paper.pdf

[6] https://www2.opengroup.org/ogsys/catalog/W133

UK Government G-Cloud definitions provide definitions of service types and criteria to be applied around data storage and processing, extraction and removal, and public, private and hybrid deployment models.

Cloud Security Alliance – Security Guidance for Critical Areas of Focus in Cloud Computing, Version 3.0 (CSA 2011). The CSA is a vendor-driven initiative, and the guidance is aimed to offer a primer for IT decision makers looking at running all or part of their IT in the cloud.

The security architect also needs to take national and international legislation into account. This is necessary not only for information transfers within the organisation, but also between organisations. Such legislation includes:

- **EU Data Protection Directive 1995** – European law that sets out criteria for processing of data. This is currently undergoing a major update, with its replacement due in 2014.

- **UK Data Protection Act 1998** – this regulates the processing of 'personal data' in the UK, that is, data which can be used to identify an individual by itself or in association with other data that is available to the person responsible for it – the 'data controller'.

- **The Official Secrets Act** – UK law covering the protection of state secrets and national security.

- **Financial services legislation, including the Markets in Financial Instruments Directive and PCI-DSS** – which apply to anyone who takes card payments or provides online commerce services, not just the finance industry.

- **Regulation of Investigatory Powers Act** – introduced in 2000 to limit the surveillance or use of individuals' information.

- **The Safe Harbor framework** – created between the EU and the US to enable exchange of personal information.

- **Computer Misuse Act** – an EU directive setting out offences with respect to computer equipment, including hacking, confidentiality breach, fraud, copyright infringement and prevention of access.

- **Copyright, patent and intellectual property law** – becoming increasingly important due to the perceived need to protect certain content – for example music, video and ebooks – from piracy, or protection of company secrets.

- **Freedom of Information Act** – UK government legislation which defines what information government departments are required to provide on request.

Your organisation may follow its own standards and have varying levels of certification, so your security architecture needs to work with these as well. Standards can have an impact on the architecture and controls involved – for example, a standard may say the location of a data item needs to be 'uniquely identifiable', which is very difficult in the case of cloud and virtualisation. Equally, it could rule out the use of remote access or the cloud altogether.

Standards and regulations can create their own minefield. For example, failure to comply with the law does not have to be down to a security weakness – potentially, quite the opposite in cases where companies have been fined for failing to disclose information in a timely fashion, due to being unable to find backup tapes. While the information may have been 'secure', it certainly was not 'available'.

SECURITY TESTING TOOLS AND TECHNIQUES

To ensure the protection of information and services, security architecture testing should not be considered in isolation, but alongside broader security testing in particular, and system and software testing in general. Again it is not the security architect's job to test everything, but to ensure that:

- the scope of tests is sufficient to ensure security test coverage;

- both testing procedures and data are kept secure;

- test metrics and reports conform to internal and external assurance requirements;

- the work has been done to an appropriate standard, following established procedures;

- results of testing and reviews have been reported correctly and honestly.

Testing costs can be burdensome, which means that security testing activities may be greeted with remarks such as, 'Is it really necessary?' The answer is to focus first on those areas, systems and services that require more stringent testing – for example, because they are part of a security domain that holds more sensitive information, they contain a particular classification of data or they need assessment to enable compliance with governance standards. If sufficient security testing budget can be found for at least these systems, then the organisation will be in a better place and may gain a clearer picture of the benefits.

To test the overall architecture, one method is to dry-run the design before it is built, for example as part of a review session with appropriate stakeholders (such as affected operations personnel and frontline staff) to ensure that what is being proposed is achievable. The scale of such a review can quickly become quite big – it is up to the architect to decide what tests would be appropriate to the mechanisms and controls being proposed, and the risks being mitigated. The law of diminishing returns most definitely applies.

Given the changing nature of the IT environment and hence its security controls, regression testing (for example, as part of a comprehensive continuous assessment process) should be seen as a standard part of any testing regime. Regression testing is where historical tests are rerun to ensure that code remains bug-free, systems work as intended and processes still have the desired result. Testing in general, and security testing in particular, can never be treated as a one-off, particularly as the effectiveness of security controls has a tendency to decay over time, making regression testing all the more important. In compliance environments, some tests will need to be carried out after every system change is implemented, to revalidate and confirm compliance.

Finally, keep in mind that test environments may be subject to the same compliance and audit conditions as live production environments, unless measures are put in place to proactively move them out of scope – for example, by ensuring that they use only anonymised data.

Testing code within applications

While security architects do not have a particular role in application development, they need to be able to understand and recommend code testing methods to ensure that the development process is sufficiently robust. Programming and software design vulnerabilities can be identified through:

- **Code review.** It is possible to conduct a line-by-line review of code, using a checklist to look for uninitiated variables and so on. However, for large quantities of code a number of free and commercial software tools now exist that can perform such functions automatically, as well as checking for more complex vulnerabilities such as buffer overruns.

- **Functional (unit) and integration testing.** This involves confirming that application elements, including compiled code, database and both server- and client-side scripts, work as expected. Again, testing suites can automate some functions, for example testing for code and SQL query injections.

Some of the above tasks can be outsourced to third parties, such as an authorised security consultancy or a commercial licensed evaluation facility (CLEF).

Testing whole systems

It is also important for the security architect to understand the methods and strategies available for security testing of business systems and online services, wherever they are situated. These include:

- **Penetration testing ('PEN testing').** That is, managed attempts to access or modify the data contained by a system or service. This can be carried out by an authorised third party such as a CLEF – in which case the target of evaluation will receive a certification certificate once any vulnerabilities have been dealt with.

- **Resilience testing.** Systems and services, together with the security controls defined to protect them (IDS and/or IPS) can also be tested for resilience against various types of failure, such as DDoS or deliberate physical attack. Failover and disaster recovery paths should also be security-tested – for example, is data moved to a failover site in a secure manner?

- **Acceptance testing.** Security should be a part of any acceptance test for both in-house and external systems, cloud-based or otherwise. It is worth considering physical aspects in acceptance testing, given that a physical weakness can circumvent controls designed into the security architecture.

- **User testing.** It is important to verify that systems are used in the expected way, as misuse may introduce new risks. For example, confidential information could be being printed off and carried in a briefcase, or downloaded onto a USB stick. So, while the system might function as required, data is still at risk.

- **Testing controls and processes.** We shall look at operational security in a moment, but before a system or service goes live, a first step is to ensure that operational procedures are security tested.

Third-party systems, applications and services need to be tested in parallel with in-house systems – this may cause challenges in terms of accessibility and indeed, authorisation – with cloud-based services for example, it is unlikely that operators would be particularly pleased about unplanned penetration testing or a DoS attack simulation!

Hand in hand with information security architecture delivery goes the need to show that security-related activities have been undertaken correctly. This has particular relevance in compliance environments such as government, healthcare or financial services, which are required to demonstrate that compliance criteria are met, not just on an ongoing basis but potentially through audits or other forms of formalised review. The mechanisms and controls that a security architect defines may themselves need to be subjected to a certification process or compliance audit, for example.

Accreditation and certification

In higher-security environments, more stringent processes may exist for authorising business systems for use. For example, a number of sectors, notably government and defence but also finance and aviation, may require that systems and services are accredited by a third-party or internal accreditor – this is usually against ISO 27000 series standards.

Some systems and services may have been pre-tested or certified, for example by way of CSA certification or ITSEC common criteria – which, as mentioned above, enable external security assessments to be compared.[7] Simpler initiatives also exist, such as the UK CESG Commercial Product Assurance (CPA) scheme (CESG 2012); note that even certified systems will still need to be integration- and acceptance-tested to ensure that they have been installed and configured correctly.

Independent accreditation brings a number of benefits, not least that it requires less effort on the part of the organisation

---

[7] http://www.commoncriteriaportal.org/files/ccfiles/CCPART1V3.1R4.pdf

to ensure systems and services meet their security policy, but also that it offers a seal of approval and promotes security overall. Note that accreditation may need to be repeated if systems are updated or new security controls are implemented.

As a final point, if the organisation has development/test environments or systems, these also need to be considered in the scope of the security architecture, and therefore as targets for testing (and potentially accreditation). This remains true if they involve VMs or cloud-hosted platforms.

SECURITY ARCHITECTURE OPERATIONS

Once systems are deployed and in operational use, how does the security architect's role change and what practical mechanisms exist to help? The security architect once again takes an advisory role, keeping an eye on management processes and activities to ensure that the initial objectives of the security architect (to reduce information risks) are fulfilled. The linkage may not always be obvious, particularly in more complex areas such as user de-provisioning, where it can be difficult to keep tabs on who has access to what on which device.

To aid the security architect, two areas of focus exist. The first is operational IT security – that is, ensuring that IT and communications staff act in a way that reduces risk rather than increases it. The second covers the policies, procedures and guidelines available to system users.

It is highly unlikely that no procedures or policies exist; more likely, however, is that existing guidance is out of date in some cases or does not take into account changes in the environment, new working practices or the evolving threat landscape. The security architect's job, therefore, is to make recommendations to bring existing operational guidance up to an appropriate level.

The security architect can also provide formal consultancy and informal advice for project and change managers, keeping an overview of IT infrastructure development, feeding guidance into strategic development and supporting the creation of roadmaps for IT systems and services as they evolve in line with business requirements.

As mentioned before, the IT security function may be required to provide input to staff training programmes, some of which may be mandated by regulatory compliance. The security architect has an important role to play in driving the content and quality of such programmes.

Operational security

Operational security management starts, like security architecture, with the organisation's strategy and overall management policy, from which a security management system and policy can be defined. As already mentioned, organisations have a number of tools and frameworks available for the management of IT systems and applications (often referred to as IT service management). These include the well-established ITIL and COBIT.

Now in its third version and an international standard (ISO 2000), ITIL was originally conceived to gather together the experiences of those working in the frontline of systems and operational management. Rather than trying to prescribe a fixed set of methods, ITIL groups a number of areas of IT management – which, indeed, covers operational security management. Security underpins both the ITIL categories of service delivery and service support, as follows:

- **service delivery** – service level management, availability management, capacity management, IT service continuity management;

- **service support** – incident management, problem management, change management, release management, configuration management.

ITIL offers direct guidance about the essential elements in a security management process, with which the security architect should become familiar:

- **Control** – put in place the structures, roles and responsibilities, procedures and processes required including how to respond to security events.

- **Plan** – define and agree SLAs, contract definitions, management policy statements and awareness training guidance.

- **Implement** – conduct due diligence and enact the defined controls to enable the secure operation of the service.

- **Monitor** – collate events, evaluate service delivery and diagnose and resolve faults to enable efficient resolution and assure compliance.

- **Improve** – review all of the above on a regular basis and report on findings and areas of improvement, to ensure existing SLAs, policies and mechanisms best meet their objectives.

- **Report** – feed back to the organisation on all areas, including against service delivery compared to expectations set in the SLA.

Implementing these steps is outside the direct purview of security architects. However, they should be able to take a view (and make recommendations) on the adequacy of the existing security management process in terms of how well it supports the security architecture, to ensure that all their good efforts to design and deploy the right security controls are not being undermined by inadequate operational management, be it security-specific or otherwise.

As well as ITIL, many organisations use COBIT, which was originally defined by the IT Governance Institute (part of the Information Systems Audit and Control Association) and which has gone through several iterations. COBIT Version 5 goes into some detail about procedures, practices and measures required for successful risk assessment, security design and operations 'across all levels of the enterprise'.

Some organisations may have a security management system and process that runs separate from the IT management; others will combine the two. In either case, security management should look to integrate with IT management. The security management system needs to be treated with the same discipline as the IT management, if it exists separately.

Operational security controls also apply to external service providers, including cloud-based services, not least as a due diligence checklist to ensure each service provider is following adequate procedures. Where a provider is not, the organisation needs to decide whether the service risk is too great to merit its continued use.

Incident investigation and remediation

Security architects may be called upon for their expertise and experience in the investigation of security incidents, the identification of causes and the assessment, planning and implementation of remediation measures – which of course may sometimes result in changes to the security architecture, such as new security controls being deployed.

Security architects may also be required to help coordinate between IT service operations/delivery staff and appropriate regulatory bodies such as the Information Commissioner's Office.

Acceptable use policy

Given the rise of BYOD and more general use of personal equipment and online services (including social networks), one policy worth highlighting is the acceptable use policy (AUP). This expresses what is considered to be acceptable employee behaviour, for example in terms of:

- Email behaviour – language used and expectations, for example where the line is drawn in terms of humorous emails, or comments/discussion about other people.

- Use of corporate storage for personal data, including audio and video (and its potential for illegal sharing).

- Social networks, in particular the need for employees to recognise that they are brand advocates for the organisation and should act accordingly.

- Hosted service access, for example use of non-corporate email services, online applications and hosted storage.

- Personal devices and their use as corporate tools, including removable storage devices such as USB sticks and external hard disk drives, and baseline security measures (such as PIN codes on smartphones).

- Corporate networks and 'tampering', for example by installing a personal Wi-Fi hub at a LAN connection point.

- Use of corporate equipment outside of the office by non-employees, such as family members, friends and associates.

Given how the above can have a significant bearing on the controls and measures stipulated by the security architecture, it is important that the security architect has the opportunity to review the AUP in the light of any controls proposed. As with other policies, less is more for the AUP – alongside the inevitable broad statements about acting as a representative of the organisation and so on, it is best to be as specific as possible about what is not acceptable.

Finally, note that a breach of the policy may also breach the employee's terms of employment and potentially constitute a disciplinary offence. Therefore, the AUP will need to be agreed by the HR department.

Vulnerability management

While it is impossible to know what security events might take place in the future and the impact they might have, organisations can nonetheless forewarn themselves about emerging threats and what actions to undertake to prepare themselves. Activities to achieve this goal are known as vulnerability management.

Enterprise organisations will normally have a regular risk review process in place – the security architect should be kept up to speed with recently identified threats, either through active participation or (if it is not a full-time role at this point) by being kept informed of any decisions.

Both proactive and reactive monitoring and compliance mechanisms, tools and processes provide a constant source of vulnerability indicators for both service delivery and the security architect.

6 CAREER PROGRESSION AND RELATED ROLES

How can budding security architects see their skills and experience develop as part of an overall career progression, and how does the role interact with others? It is improbable that a security architect will come to the position 'cold', with no prior experience – indeed, much information security knowledge is common to multiple roles. Given how the security architect role brings together security and IT architecture, it is more likely that it will either involve a security professional who now needs to take a more architectural view, or an IT architect who is having to consider security aspects of the technology environment. The security architect will in general previously have been an IT or security professional already operating at a senior level.

Based on how much experience a person will need to bring to bear and the level at which he or she will need to operate, we can consider 'gradings' of security architect as follows:

- **Practitioners** represent security requirements and interests in the design and implementation of IT architectures. They typically support a single project, information system, service or business unit, and may have no experience as information security practitioners or IT architects beyond these activities.

- **Senior practitioners** guide and enable the design and implementation of secure IT architectures. They typically work with clients or service owners to contribute to the success of a programme or multiple projects. They have sufficient experience to handle significant complexity and require little supervision.

- **Lead practitioners** provide input to enterprise architectures to ensure that strategic security requirements are incorporated. Typically, they influence the senior information risk officer's area of responsibility, the corporate investment portfolio or corporate governance to optimise the balance between information security and strategic business objectives.

These gradings reflect the levels of responsibility defined by the Skills Framework for the Information Age (SFIA) Foundation, set up in 2003 to provide a standardised definition of IT skills development and adopted by BCS. Its SFIAplus guidance provides seven levels of skills, from being able to follow guidance at Level 1, to setting corporate strategy at Level 7 – each measured according to criteria of autonomy, influence, complexity of the role and business skills. The senior practitioner level of security architect corresponds broadly to SFIAplus Responsibility Level 4 ('Enable') and Knowledge Level K4 ('Analyse').

CERTIFICATION AND CONTINUOUS PROFESSIONAL DEVELOPMENT

A security architect may seek to gain formal qualification via a certification programme, for example as part of a continuous professional development (CPD) process. Certification enables a consolidation of skills and experience, supported by appropriate training to fill any gaps. Meanwhile CPD offers a progression route, from foundation level to intermediate and practitioner level, enabling security architects to build upon existing skills and guiding their individual learning process.

The CESG Certification for IA Professionals is a certification scheme reflecting the practitioner, senior practitioner and lead practitioner gradings described above. The Institute of Information Security Professionals (IISP) builds on these levels to define a number of groups of security skills, of which security architecture is one. The IISP's skills framework requires security architects to demonstrate up to Level 3 (Skilful Application) competence, possessing 'a more detailed understanding and application of knowledge to demonstrate how the IT professional can be effective in that area'. That is, practical, hands-on experience is fundamental.

Other beneficial accreditations include formal qualifications such as Qualified Security Assessor, Cisco Certified Security Associate, and Microsoft Certified Security Professional. As we have seen, skills and experience learned from fields including enterprise architecture, IT and application architecture, contract management, project management and software testing can also benefit the role, so qualifications and certifications in these areas will not be wasted.

INTERFACE AND DEPENDENCIES

Throughout this book we have seen how the security architect needs to coordinate and liaise, to request and review, and to influence and provide guidance to individuals across the business. They could be acting individually, or as part of a team; equally, the role may be full-time, part-time, or performed on a consulting basis.

To achieve this end, the security architect will need to engage with a wide variety of roles:

- **The board of directors,** with whom security respon-sibility ultimately lies. While the security architect might not expect to engage daily with board members, the latter group should be aware of ongoing activities and progress, and be prepared to review and sign off security solutions proposed as part of a well-defined security architecture.

- **Enterprise, systems and solutions architects,** whose job it is to model the business and create appropriate architectures for technology solutions. Given that security architecture can be seen as a subset of enterprise architecture, the security architect will need to work closely with other architects at every stage.

- **The chief technology officer,** who often acts as the ultimate point of responsibility for systems architecture decisions and who may oversee policies around IT approaches, toolsets and so on – for example, the organisation's use of open source. The security architect will need to coordinate with the chief technology officer to ensure that proposals for security controls are congruent with the organisation's technology choices.

- **The chief information officer,** who has overall responsibility for the IT systems in place and, therefore, for their security. The security architect can engage with the chief information officer as a first point of contact when starting the information gathering process, and will continue to liaise throughout the security architecture development life cycle.

- **Corporate and departmental security officers,** whose task it is to define and ensure the technical and potentially physical security of the organisation. From the outset, the security architect will benefit from the hands-on experience of security officers to build a picture of existing corporate security policy and how it has been implemented.

- **Senior information risk owners, and security and information risk advisors,** who are responsible for defining the levels of risk associated with specific information assets. These roles provide an invaluable source of information concerning the risks, threats and vulnerabilities currently driving security policy and, indeed, any perceived gaps in implementation.

- **Compliance officers and information assurance auditors,** who provide guidance around the regulations and legislation with which the organisation needs to comply, oversee the auditing process and make recommendations as to countermeasures for any issues uncovered. The security architect will not only use such inputs during information gathering, but also need to coordinate with these roles to ensure the resulting security architecture meets compliance and assurance requirements.

Many organisations will already have some kind of coordinating body or steering group in place to consider security issues and to ensure recommendations are implemented. The name is less important than its function and membership – most, if not all of the above stakeholders should be represented, as well as representatives from lines of business, HR and finance. While this overhead might seem unnecessary, involving those whose work is directly impacted is a major precursor to successful security architecture implementation. In the worst-case scenario, security measures might be implemented that are perceived as unnecessary and/or bureaucratic, the consequence of which is that the measures are undermined or worked around by management or staff.

Note that while some security-related roles (including that of the security architect) are defined specifically, not all organisations will apply the definitions to the letter, particularly outside the government sector. Just because a role exists does not mean that the 'standard' tasks are being done, or vice versa. Therefore, in order to liaise fully, it is up to the security architect to look beyond titles and consider the nature of the roles. Indeed, it can be seen as a valid part of any security assessment to identify who in the organisation has which roles and responsibilities, and to build these into architecture activities.

As mentioned in Chapter 4, given the inherent complexities in defining and deploying security architecture, a clear element of the security architect's role is to have good interpersonal skills. Communication is central to the job, as the security architect needs to be able not only to define appropriate measures, but also undertake the 'internal sale' – that is, convince others sufficiently of their necessity that they will be prepared to back them.

The security architect may also have a wider remit to influence security architecture practices outside the organisation – for example, through participation in working groups, both within and outside the public sector. A spin-off benefit is gaining education on new threats and their mitigations, as well as gaining increased influence within the organisation, which can itself help achieve the goals of security architecture.

7 A DAY IN THE LIFE OF A SECURITY ARCHITECT

Security architecture, for many organisations, will always be a work in progress. And, as mentioned, the security architect's role might not be full-time – it could be either an external consultant working part-time or one of many roles being carried out by a single person. So, how might a security architect's day map out? While each day is likely to be different, it has the potential to involve some or all of the following:

- On arrival, a review of email alerts and newsletters should indicate if any new issues have arisen, which are checked against existing systems and services. There may also be some advice to give, feedback to send or documents to review. The security architect receives no small amount of communication and requests for advice, and needs to respond accordingly.

- Once any urgent communications have been dealt with, the security architect can turn to the task in hand – the security architecture itself. Depending on the scope and what stage this has reached, he or she will be pulling together materials and producing documents and plans relating to assessment, design or deployment of security controls, or writing guidance for practitioners and employees.

- Consultancy and advice requested by the change programme manager requires a response, and there are several project managers asking for guidance, two of whom need face-to-face meetings to discuss their urgent requirements. Then someone from the business needs a quick answer to a question about access for a third-party organisation – it never ends!

- After a bite of lunch, it is time for a progress meeting. This involves senior members of the security architecture steering group – not all of whom agree with the proposed controls, particularly as one system is reaching the end of its life. The resulting decision is to decommission the system more quickly, saving money that can be spent elsewhere.

- Unfortunately, the security architect does not have an assistant, so it falls to him or her to write up the notes for the meeting. This is interspersed with an email exchange with the procurement department who want to confirm some details about a VPN appliance to be deployed for home workers.

- Late afternoon, a security awareness session is planned for the sales department. The security architect presents recent progress and explains the thinking behind the latest version of the acceptable use policy, which includes recommendations for use of personal devices. The meeting runs on, as the sales teams have many questions, but it seems to go well.

- Before leaving for the day, the security architect checks his or her email one last time. A new threat has been uncovered which could affect users of a certain system, depending on the software version. Fortunately this time, following checks with the system administrator, it turns out that the system was recently updated so no major changes are required – this time.

With a wry smile, the security architect heads home in the knowledge that if anything else comes up, he or she can always be contacted on his or her smartphone.

8   CONCLUSION

Over the past decade, we have seen the nature of computing change. Whereas the model was once largely based on technology stacks with varying degrees of integration, today's hyper-distributed approaches, working practices and personal behaviours require a very different kind of thinking. In security terms, this means moving away from defence-in-depth protection of individual corporate systems, to protecting information assets and services wherever, and however, they are being accessed.

While this more architectural starting point is impacting information security in much the same way as other IT disciplines, the field of IT security architecture is relatively new. As a result, not all organisations may be convinced as to why security architecture is necessary, particularly given that it comes with a price tag. The simple answer is that cyber-criminals are benefiting from the same technological advances as everyone else. As attacks become increasingly complex and targeted, no organisation should leave its security posture to chance.

A security architecture cannot exist in a vacuum – rather, it is an overlay onto the enterprise, IT or solution architecture, which ensures business risks are mitigated and compliance requirements are met in accordance with corporate strategy. Given the breadth of skills required, it will not be possible for people coming to security architecture for the first time to do everything in this book – some areas require substantial experience. However, we hope it provides a suitable foundation upon which such skills can be developed.

Above all, the security architect should expect the unexpected, and respond pragmatically. Consider the recent scenario where a piece of paper, held in a TV presenter's hand, contained a potentially incriminating list of people (some of whom later sued for damages) – could this threat have been mitigated in advance? Similarly, an overbearing authentication system may cause staff to print out and photocopy confidential information, creating additional sources of risk. Information security can sometimes feel like a game of 'splat the rat', where new threats emerge even as existing threats are dealt with: it is up to the security architect to ensure he or she offers solutions without creating additional problems.

Against such a complex and dynamically changing background, in addition to technical knowledge and experience the security architect will require a high level of diligence, pragmatism and interpersonal skills. While the problems may be technological, a major part of the solution will come down to how well the security architect understands the needs of the organisation, and the ability to define workable solutions that senior decision makers are prepared to sign off.

With this in mind, here's wishing you the best of luck in all your security architecture projects.

APPENDIX
SECURITY ARCHITECTURE
DOCUMENT REVIEW
CHECKLIST

In Chapter 3 we introduced the security architecture document, which may exist as a stand-alone document or as part of broader IT or enterprise architecture documentation. The document cannot be exhaustive. However, when reviewing the finished document, reviewers should be able to answer the following questions:

- Is the scope correct and complete, with all relevant systems, services and information assets identified?

- Are out-of-scope systems, services and information assets clearly stated?

- Are all information types classified according to the needs of the organisation?

- Are all potential locations identified and mapped to access devices in use at each location – desktops, laptops, tablets, smartphones and so on?

- Is a mapping provided between existing information types, the physical environment and both physical and logical elements of the IT architecture?

- Are existing threats, vulnerabilities and existing weaknesses clearly, comprehensively yet succinctly expressed? Note that the document should not become a long-winded treatise on risk!

- Are proposed security domains, access controls and authentication mechanisms clearly defined in a way that addresses the threats and vulnerabilities?

- Are all communications paths treated (e.g. with encryption) to ensure confidentiality?

- Are costs realistic, reflecting not just up-front expense but training, ongoing operational management and so on?

- Are roles and responsibilities clearly defined, both internally and externally?

- Is the result auditable to ensure the overall IT systems architecture can be verified as compliant?

- Are the applicable regulatory and standards compliance criteria being met?

- Is the proposed solution fit for purpose and future safe, and can it be operated to the required level of security as a function of business as usual?

REFERENCES

BCS (2012) 'Reference Model for BCS Certificates in Enterprise and Solution Architecture, Version 4.0'. http://certifications. bcs.org/upload/pdf/sd-esa-reference-model.pdf (accessed 4 June 2014).

Cabinet Office (2013) 'Guidance: Government Security Classifications'. https://www.gov.uk/government/uploads/ system/uploads/attachment_data/file/251480/Government-Security-Classifications-April-2014.pdf (accessed 4 June 2014).

Carr, N. (2003) 'Does IT matter?' *Harvard Business Review*, May. http://hbr.org/2003/05/it-doesnt-matter/ar/1 (accessed 5 May 2014).

Cloud Security Alliance (2011) 'Security Guidance for Critical Areas of Focus in Cloud Computing v3.0'. https://downloads. cloudsecurityalliance.org/initiatives/guidance/csaguide. v3.0.pdf (accessed 22 November 2013).

Cloud Security Alliance (2013) 'Cloud Security Alliance Cloud Controls Matrix'. https://cloudsecurityalliance.org/research/ ccm/ (accessed 22 November 2013).

CESG (2012) 'Commercial Product Assurance (CPA) Scheme'. http://www.cesg.gov.uk/servicecatalogue/Product-Assurance/CPA/Pages/CPA.aspx (accessed 25 April 2014).

Department for Business Innovation and Skills (2013) '2013 Information Security Breaches Survey'. http://www.pwc.co.uk/ assets/pdf/cyber-security-2013-technical-report.pdf (accessed 4 June 2014).

Scammell, T. (2003) 'Security architecture: One practitioner's view'. *Information Systems Control Journal*, Vol. 1. http://www. isaca.org/Journal/Past-Issues/2003/Volume-1/Documents/ jpdf031-SecurityArchitecture.pdf (accessed 1 November 2013).

Taylor, A. (ed.), Alexander, D., Finch, A. and Sutton, D. (2013) *Information Security Management Principles* (2nd edn). BCS: Swindon.

FURTHER READING

Basil, K. et al. (2013) OpenStack Security Guide. OpenStack Foundation. http://docs.openstack.org/sec/ (accessed 1 November 2013).

BCS (2014) 'Professional Certification Roles Explained'. http://certifications.bcs.org/category/16266 (accessed 5 May 2014).

Blue Coat Systems (2013) 'Security Empowers Business – Unlock the Power of a Protected Enterprise'. http://www.bluecoat.com/documents/download/2fde0803-8a2b-47fb-8507-2ad7a52374da/e1b1b8c2-8128-40f8-a72b-0289b53d78b3 (accessed 5 May 2014).

Cabinet Office (2011) 'Cyber Security Strategy'. https://www.gov.uk/government/publications/cyber-security-strategy (accessed 29 November 2013).

Cabinet Office (2013) 'Security policy framework'. https://www.gov.uk/government/publications/security-policy-framework (accessed 29 November 2013).

CESG (2012) 'New Certification Scheme announced for IA Professionals – Press Release'. CESG. http://www.cesg.gov.uk/News/Pages/New-IA-Certification-pages.aspx (accessed 5 May 2014).

Dyke, J. (2007) 'The Open University M226 SFIAplus® Framework Guide'. Open University. http://mct.open.ac.uk/80256EE9006B7FB0/(httpAssets)/D5ACA267626B3A51802573270034BEFE/$file/SFIABookletProdFinal.pdf (accessed 5 May 2014).

European Commission MEMO/14/186 (March 2014), Progress on EU Data Protection Reform Now Irreversible Following European Parliament Vote. http://europa.eu/rapid/press-release_MEMO-14-186_en.htm (accessed 26 April 2014).

Fujitsu Limited Information Security Center (2007) 'Fujitsu Enterprise Security Architecture'. http://jp.fujitsu.com/solutions/safety/secure/concept/esa/files/ESA5010P.pdf (accessed 14 October 2013).

Furgel, I. (2008) 'Security Domain Separation as Prerequisite for Business Flexibility'. http://www.commoncriteriaportal.org/iccc/9iccc/pdf/C2405.pdf (14 January 2014).

IISP (2007) 'Our Skills Framework'. https://www.iisp.org/imis15/iisp/About_Us/Our_Skills_Framework/iisp/About_Us/Our_Skills_Framework.aspx?hkey=6a996e64-4c90-4892-bb7e-b3d6e5dff3d5 (accessed 5 May 2014).

Information Commissioner's Office (no date) 'Data Protection Principles'. http://ico.org.uk/for_organisations/data_protection/the_guide/the_principles (26 April 2014).

Information Systems Audit and Control Association (2009) 'The ISACA Risk IT Framework'. http://www.isaca.org/Knowledge-Center/Research/ResearchDeliverables/Pages/The-Risk-IT-Framework.aspx (accessed 26 April 2014).

Information Systems Audit and Control Association (2012) 'ISACA Issues COBIT 5 for Information Security'. http://www.isaca.org/About-ISACA/Press-room/News-Releases/2012/Pages/ISACA-Issues-COBIT-5-for-Information-Security.aspx (accessed 5 May 2014).

Information Systems Audit and Control Association (2012) 'COBIT 5 for information Security Introduction'. http://www.isaca.org/COBIT/Documents/COBIT-5-for-Information-Security-Introduction.pdf (accessed 29 November 2013).

ITIL (2011) 'Core Study Material for ITIL® Qualifications'. http://www.itil-officialsite.com/nmsruntime/saveasdialog.aspx?lID=950&sID=56 (accessed 26 April 2014).

Jericho Forum (2011) 'The Jericho Forum® Identity, Entitlement, and Access Management (IdEA) Commandments'. https://collaboration.opengroup.org/jericho/Jericho%20Forum%20Identity%20Commandments%20v1.0.pdf (accessed 29 November 2013).

The Open Group (Dec 2011) 'Security Principles for Cloud and SOA'. https://www2.opengroup.org/ogsys/jsp/publications/PublicationDetails.jsp?publicationid=12511 (accessed 14 October 2013).

Payment Card Industry (2013) 'Payment Card Industry Data Security Standard Issue 3.0'. https://www.pcisecuritystandards.org/security_standards/documents.php (accessed 26 April 2014).

SANS Institute (2002) 'One Approach to Enterprise Security Architecture'. http://www.sans.org/reading-room/whitepapers/policyissues/approach-enterprise-security-architecture-504 (accessed 14 October 2013).

SANS institute (2013) 'Critical Controls for Effective Cyber Defense Version 4.1'. http://www.sans.org/critical-security-controls/ (accessed 14 January 2014).

Schneier, B. (2000) *Secrets and Lies: Digital Security in a Networked World*. John Wiley & Sons: New York.

SFIA (2013) 'SFIA and Grading'. http://www.sfia-online.org/about-sfia/sfia-and-grading/ (accessed 6 May 2014).

Vilcinskas, M. (2000) 'The Need for a Security Architecture. Security Entities Building Block Architecture'. http://technet.microsoft.com/en-us/library/cc723497.aspx (accessed 1 November 2013).

Willson, N. (2013) 'Architecture Case Study – Part 1'. http://nigesecurityguy.wordpress.com/2013/06/28/architecture-case-study-part-1/ (accessed 1 November 2013).

INDEX

Where is your career going?

Map it out with our free personal development plan

pdp.bcs.org

BCS, The Chartered Institute for IT, First Floor Block D North Star House North Star Avenue Swindon SN2 1FA
T +44 (0) 1793 417 424 Online enquiries www.bcs.org/contact **www.bcs.org**
© The British Computer Society (Registered charity no. 292786) 2014
If you require this document in accessible format please call +44 (0) 1793 417 600

CPSIA information can be obtained at www.ICGtesting.com
Printed in the USA
LVOW04s0016271214

420530LV00003B/130/P